INDIA'S NUCLEAR MIGHT

Dr. Om Parkash Pahuja

M.Sc. (Physics), Ph.D.

Ocean Books Pvt. Ltd.

ISO 9001:2015 Publishers

Published by
Ocean Books (P) Ltd.
4/19 Asaf Ali Road,
New Delhi-110 002 (INDIA)
e-mail: info@oceanbooks.in

ISBN 978-81-8430-138-0
INDIA'S NUCLEAR MIGHT
by Dr. Om Parkash Pahuja

Edition
2025

Price
₹ 300.00 (Rupees Three Hundred only)

Printed at
Yash Printographics, Noida

India's Nuclear Doctrine

"India's nuclear weapons are solely for deterrence and that India will pursue a policy of 'retaliation only.' India 'will not be the first to initiate a nuclear first strike, but will respond with punitive retaliation,' and that decisions to authorise the use of nuclear weapons would be made by the Prime Minister or his 'designated successor(s)'."

— released by India's National Security Advisory Board on August 17, 1999.

INDIA'S NUCLEAR MIGHT

Introduction

This book contains the elementary unclassified information which a common man of a country, particularly a Nuclear Weapon State like India, needs to know.

The basics of nuclear power, the nuclear energy necessary for the country's Industrial Power, are the subject matter of first two chapters.

The third chapter gives the amusing history of discovery of the Nuclear Chain Reaction which led to the making of horrible Weapons of Mass Destruction (WMDs), as well as Nuclear Reactors for the electrical power. This chapter also describes the types and designing of various nuclear bombs, horrible effects on a nuclear blast and extremely painful sufferings of the survivors. Also described in this chapter are delivery systems of nuclear weapons, nuclear arsenal of nuclear powers, and estimated cost of nuclear weaponisation.

The fourth and fifth chapters give the history of India's nuclear bomb and the bomb-makers, the Shakti Operations at Pokhran and Prime Minister's announcement of India becoming a Nuclear Power State. It also describes India's achievements in the different fields of bomb-making; nuclear-capable missiles, bomber planes, submarines and war-frigates; thus completing a Nuclear Triad essential for country's foolproof defence. Other topics included in this chapter are on Nuclear Command Authority of India, its present Nuclear Arsenal, its future needs and the estimated cost of India's nuclear weaponisation for Minimum Deterrence, and its Security Concerns.

Sixth chapter tells why and how India's nuclear program is blessed by Lord Buddha—the torch-bearer of world's peace. Next two chapters give the account of India's efforts for nuclear disarmament and the way it faced the economic sanctions imposed on India by the developed countries.

The last chapter gives a lucid short-story describing the secrecy, patience, dedication and perfection with which great Indian scientists and engineers completed the 'Mission Shakti' entrusted to them by their beloved and respected Prime Minister.

—Om Parkash Pahuja

Few Words

It was Buddha Purnima, May 11, 1998, the day when Apostle of peace—Lord Buddha achieved 'Nirvan', the Seismographs at the laboratories of spying centres in different parts of the world, recorded the simultaneous explosion of three Indian Nuclear Bombs. This stunned the world and exposed one of America's biggest intelligence failure. But all over India, particularly throughout Rajasthan and villages around Pokhran, people were talking of nothing but of India's tryst of a different kind. There was dancing in the streets, fire works and distribution of sweets by the people even in the rural areas.

Joining my countrymen on this festival of national pride, I felt the need to educate them about the scientific details of this great Indian experiment. I wished our people, who now belong to a proud country and a Nuclear Weapon State, should know about the nuclear Chain Reaction, nuclear bomb making, their delivery systems, nuclear war strategy, the social and military fallout of the explosions, the disarmament and the problem of facing economic sanctions by advanced countries.

So I wrote my first book, *India: a Nuclear Weapon State.* I thank my readers for appreciating the book very much and they suggested to publish its Hindi version, which I did gladly. Later, I felt the readers deserve more revelations and details on the subject. Therefore, on the basis of my collections from daily newspapers, such as *The Hindustan Times, The Indian Express,* weeklies

India Today and *Organiser*, the different Wikipedia from the internet etc. I revised the subject matter of my first book thoroughly and added some new topics. The result is before you, in the form of the book, *India's Nuclear Might,*

Though I have tried to present the book in a simple language, yet the reader with little scientific background may find the first chapter, being purely scientific, a bit difficult. Such a reader may start reading from the chapter 2. After finishing the last chapter, he can come back to chapter 1. With this. I hope, like my earlier book, the knowledge-seekers will enjoy and welcome my humble presentation this time also.

—Om Parkash Pahuja

Contents

1

Basics of Nuclear Power

> **"Fission and Fusion have had such a great impact on our culture that many of us feel that very survival of civilization as we know it is dangerously hanging by a thread."**
>
> ***—Jay Orear, in his book 'Fundamental Physics'***
>
> **"The bomb has given us a few years of grace without war and now it promises us a millenium of oblivion."**
>
> ***— E. B. White***

In order to understand the world of nuclear weapons, we must make ourselves familiar with some basic 'terms and 'concepts' frequently occurring in this field.

Atomic Energy: ***It is the energy produced by atoms.***

The Atom: The atom is the fundamental building block of all stuff, or what scientists like to call 'matter'. Every single object is composed of atoms. Our body is made of many, many individual atoms. There are so many different types of atoms. In fact, there are over 100. The different types are called elements. Examples of such elements are Hydrogen, Oxygen, Iron, Copper, Silver, Gold etc.

The Atom is a basic unit of matter that consists of a dense, central nucleus surrounded by a cloud of nagatively charged electrons. Electrons orbit the nucleus from outside in electron shells that have different shapes at different distances from the nucleus.

The atoms are the smallest particles of matter with definite properties and cannot be seen directly even through a microscope. An Individual atom is very small. In fact, the smallest type of atom , Hydrogen, has a diameter of 10^{-8} cm.This means that if the hydrogen atom is of the size of a soccer ball, then a soccer ball would be 6450 km (4008 miles) high.

The concept of an atom as an indivisible component of matter was first proposed by early Indian Scientists. They called it **'Paramanu'**. The **'Atom'** is the Greek equivalent of Paramanu.

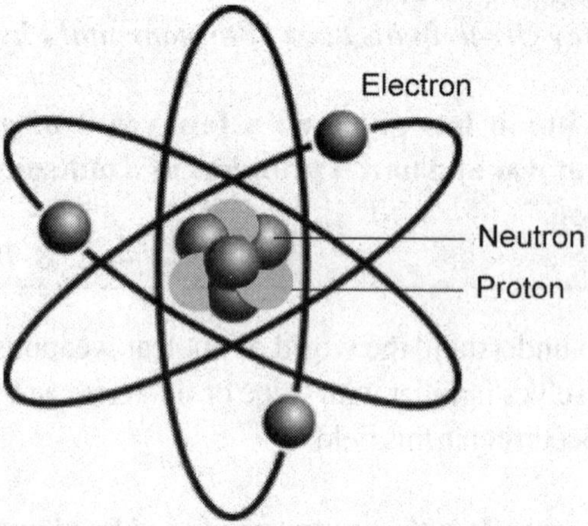

Lithium Atom

Nucleus: The atomic nucleus contains a mix of two types of particles called protons and neutrons, except in case of hydrogen-1, which is the only stable nucleus with no neutrons.

Protons, particles, each with a positive (+) charge and a mass of 1.6726×10^{-27}kg (This amount of mass is called atomic mass unit, AMU).

Neutrons: These particles do not have any charge, they are electrically neutral and each has mass of 1.6929×10^{-27} kg, almost the same as that of proton.

Since protons and neutrons are very similar, except that proton carries one unit positive charge while neutron is electrically neutral, and also both are the part of the **nucleus**, we use the term nucleon for either a proton or a neutron.

Electrons, each with a negative (–) charge and a very less mass of 9.11×10^{-31} kg, that is only 1/1836 the mass of a proton.

Atomic Number: In a stable atom, the number of electrons is equal to the number of protons. This number is called atomic number and is denoted by the letter 'Z'.

Mass Number of an element is equal to the total number of nucleons (sum of protons and neutrons) in its atom and is normally denoted by the letter 'A'.

The Forces between Nucleons: There are three types of forces influencing nucleons to keep them bound within the nucleus.

(i) The gravitational force is usual attractive force taking place between any two material bodies.
(ii) The Coulombian force is the electrostatic force which is of repulsive nature between the positively charged protons.
(iii) The nuclear force is again the attractive force between the nucleons.

While gravitational and Coulombian forces vary inversely as the square of the distance between the nucleons, the nuclear force are not effective when the distance between the two nucleons is more than 10^{-15} cm. At the same time nuclear force within this range is much stronger than other two – about 35 times stronger than the Coulombian force and 10^{38} times stronger than the gravitational force. Therefore, it is predominantly the nuclear force which keeps the nucleons within the nucleus tightly bound together.

Binding Energy: The force responsible for keeping the nucleons bound together is called binding energy of the nucleus. In physics we customarily use energy (E) as unit of mass (m) in accordance to the Einstein mass-energy equivalence $E = mC^2$, where C is the velocity of light. Actually the binding energy is the energy needed for a nucleon to escape the nucleus.

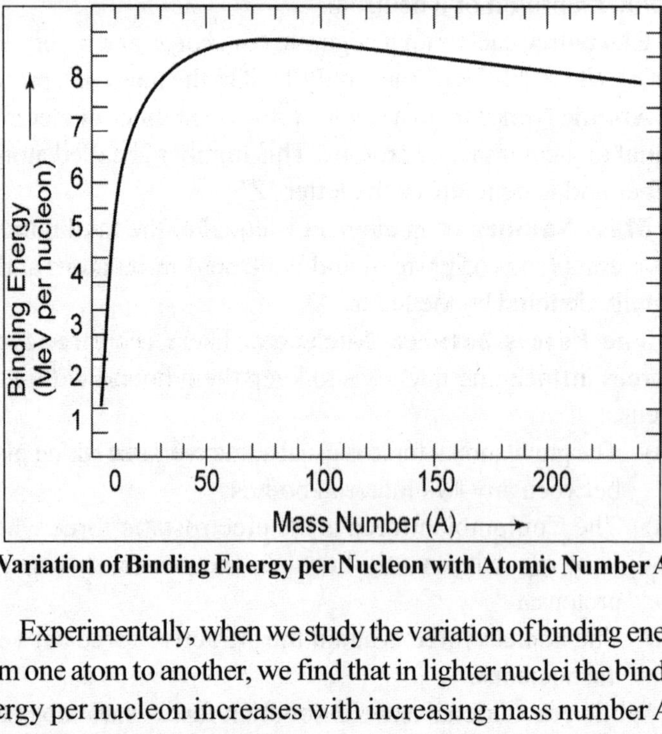

Variation of Binding Energy per Nucleon with Atomic Number A

Experimentally, when we study the variation of binding energy from one atom to another, we find that in lighter nuclei the binding energy per nucleon increases with increasing mass number A of the nucleus. But this variation is not linear. Actually, (see the graph above) nuclei with $A < 80$ are the most tightly bound. That is, the binding energy per nucleon goes on increasing as we go from lighter nuclei to heavier ones. For nuclei heavier than this (for $A > 80$), the binding energy per nucleon gradually decreases with increasing A.

This behavior of binding energy can be understood by remembering that the attractive nuclear force is of short range. Since in heavier nuclei the outer nucleons are at larger distances from inner ones, the attractive nuclear force is decreased while the repulsive electrostatic force is increased. So the net attractive force which binds them is decreased. Therefore such nuclei are less tightly bound.

The two consequences of this behavior of the binding energy are two types of nuclear reactions– **Nuclear Fission** and **Nuclear Fusion.**

We must know that the **nuclear reaction** is a process in which nuclei or nuclear particles interact, resulting in products different from the initial ones.

Nuclear Fission: If a heavy nucleus like Uranium is somehow split into two smaller nuclei (almost of equal mass), we find that the total mass of these smaller nuclei is less than that of their parent nucleus. The difference of masses (about 0.1% of the original mass) of the parent and the product is liberated in the form of energy. ***The splitting of a heavy nucleus into smaller nuclei with the liberation of energy is called Nuclear Fission, and the energy thus liberated is called Fission Energy***. The energy of the Atom Bomb and of a Nuclear Reactor is the energy released in nuclear Fission.

Though spontaneous fission is permitted by the energy conservation laws, yet its probability to occur in naturally occurring nuclei is extremely small. On the other hand if a heavy nucleus, say Uranium, U (A=235) is hit by a neutron, n, its probability to fission increases and at one stage it may split into two pieces Barium, Ba (A=141) and Krypton, Kr (A=92) and three free electrons. The mass difference between Uranium nucleus and the fission products is released in the form of energy.

The energy released in average U^{235} fission is 200 MeV (Million electron Volt). To assess the enormity of this energy, we calculate the released energy when one gram of U^{235} fissions. This comes out to be the same that is obtained on burning 300 tones of coal. The actual nuclear reaction is written as

$$_{92}U^{235} + _0n^1 \longrightarrow _{56}Ba^{141} + _{36}Kr^{92} + 3_0n^1 + \text{Energy}$$

and is depicted pictorially as

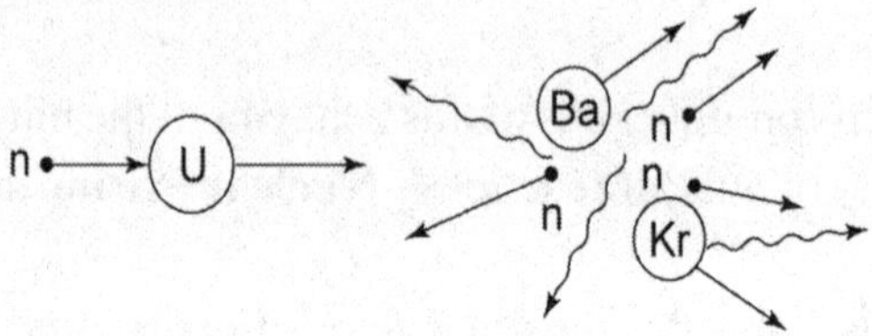

The Nuclear Chain Reaction: We have seen above that every fission releases two or three neutrons. If at least one of these three neutrons manages to induce fission in another Uranium nucleus, the process is self sustaining and gives rise to a Chain Reaction. If each fission releases two more neutrons, as depicted in diagram, then the number of fission doubles at each stage. In that case, in 10 stages these are $2^{10} = 1024$ fissions and in 80 stages, about 6×10^{23} fissions. This chain-reaction, if uncontrolled gives nothing but a ***Nuclear Weapon (the bomb).***

Nuclear Power: The nuclear power is the electricity produced by using nuclear reactions in nuclear reactors.

Critical Mass: For the fission to take place, we need that the mass of the fissile material should be greater than a critical value. To understand this, let us take one kilogram of either Uranium (U^{235}) or Plutonium (Pu^{239}). This is about the size of a golf ball. If inside this ball, one of the nuclei is made to fission, the fast moving (with a speed more than 10^8m/s) neutrons produced would leave the metal sphere without causing a second fission because of the small size of the ball. If we increase the mass and hence the size of the ball, the possibility of at least one of the three neutrons produced in the fission to be entrapped to strike another nucleus increases. *The mass of the metal at which this happens is called Critical Mass.* Thus the chain reaction is a mass reaction. In the sub critical mass there is no chain reaction, while in a super critical mass chain reaction starts spontaneously and is sustained.

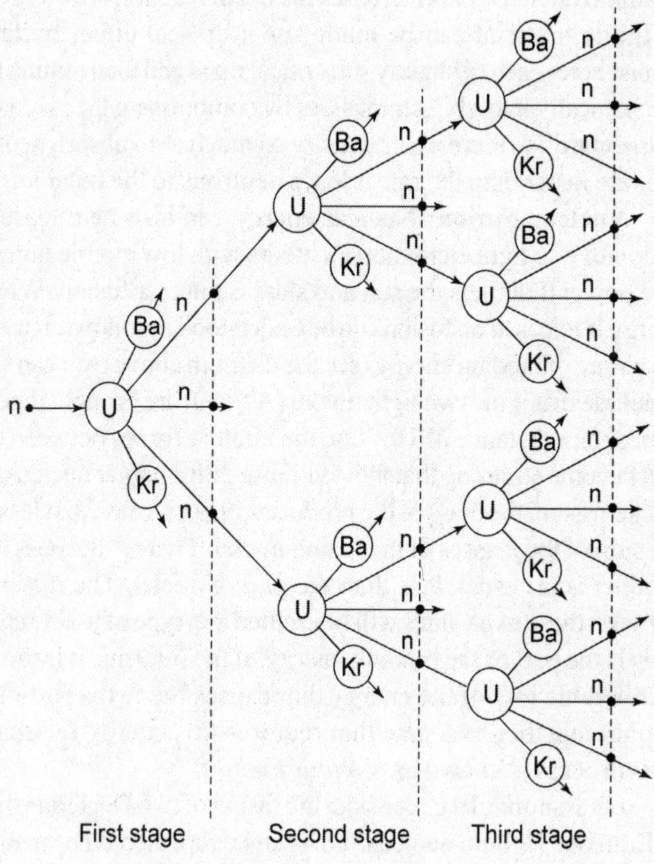

First three stages of Chain Reaction

By controlling the number of fissioned nuclei, we can control the chain reaction and hence energy released by it. This is the underlying principle of a Nuclear Reactor.

Theoretically, the critical mass for pure U^{235} is 1 kg, but because of impurities this value is 50 kg. Similarly, the practical value of critical mass for Pu^{239} is 16 kg. If we use a thick layer of U^{238} around U^{239}, the critical mass reduces to 10 kg. Actually U^{238}layer does not allow the librated neutrons to escape without hitting a

Uranium nucleus. This increases the chain reaction. The assembly of fissile material can be made super critical either by taking hemispheres each of slightly sub critical mass and then joining them mechanically into a bigger mass, or by compressing the given mass momentarily to increase its density so much as to absorb neutrons at a rate faster than the rate it loses neutrons to the outside

Nuclear Fusion: Nuclear energy can also be released by fusion of two light elements (elements with low atomic number). The power that fuels the sun and stars is nuclear fusion. Why the energy is released on fusion can be understood as follows. Knowing the nature of binding energy (see the diagram above), we can easily conclude that if the two light nuclei ($A \ll 80$) are brought together, as near as a distance of 10^{-15}cm, the nuclear forces between them will become so strong that they will fuse into a bigger nucleus. But, unlike fission, the mass of the product will not be more but less than the sum of the masses of the fusing nuclei. That is, the mass of the product is, as usual, less than the parent nuclei. The difference between these two values will be emitted as a type of usable energy. This is the part of the binding energy of the nucleus. It is the non-recoverable loss of the energy that causes the fused particles to remain together in a state that requires this energy to separate. This process is known as *Nuclear Fusion*.

For example, let us consider the fusion of two Deuterium nuclei to form one Helium nucleus. This can be represented by a nuclear reaction as,

$$_1H^2 + {}_1H^2 \longrightarrow \text{(fusion)} \longrightarrow 2H_e^{\ 4} + \text{Energy}$$

To calculate the energy released in the above reaction we proceed like this: On a scale where the mass of Deuterium nucleus is 2 amu, the observed value of Helium mass is 3.975 amu. Thus, the mass difference between the fused nuclei and product nucleus is ($2 \times 2 - 3.975 =$) 0.025amu. Since 1amu = 931MeV of energy, the energy released will be $0.025 \times 931 =$ 23.275MeV.

Similarly in a Hydrogen bomb, Deuterium and Tritium nuclei are fused to form a helium nucleus and one neutron,

$$_{1}H^{2} + {}_{1}H^{3} \longrightarrow \text{(fusion)} \longrightarrow {}_{2}He^{4} + {}_{0}n^{1} + \text{Energy}$$

Unlike nuclear fission, there is no limit on the amount of the fusion that can occur.

The Atom Bomb: When chain reaction starts in a sphere of fissile material, the burning of the material is complete within no time. This is because neutrons travel with velocities greater than 10^8 cm per second, a supercritical assembly can be all used up (blown up) in much less than a thousandth of a second. This highly explosive device is called an Atom Bomb.

MK-6 Nuclear Bomb

One of the metals which may be used in Atom Bomb is Uranium. Ordinarily available Uranium contains three types of atoms differing in mass, called its Isotopes. The percentage of each isotope in an ordinarily available sample is U^{238}:99.280; U^{235}: 0.714; and U^{234}: 0.006. Out of these, U^{235} is fissile and fissions with slow neutrons, and U^{238} is fertile, that is, can be made fissile when bombarded by fast neutrons,

$$_{92}U^{238} + {}_{0}n^{1} \text{ (fast)} \longrightarrow {}_{92}U^{239}$$

The product $_{92}U^{239}$ is actually another well known fissile metal called Plutonium. The actual fuel used is enriched Uranium – a sample with 3% of U^{235}. The enrichment of Uranium can be done by a technical process called Gas Diffusion Process.

The Hydrogen Bomb: The fusion of two Deuterium nuclei into Helium nucleus (which gives rise to Hydrogen bomb) cannot take place at room temperature. The electrostatic repulsion between two Deuterium nuclei at this temperature does not permit them to get within the range of each other's (short range) attractive nuclear forces. But, this type of nuclear reaction, as we know, has been taking place on the Sun where the temperature is very high, about 10^7 degree Kelvin. This is called the *Critical Temperature*. In fusion, therefore, we need to manage the critical temperature instead of critical mass. The nuclear reactions which require the temperature of the order of millions of degrees are called Thermo Nuclear Reactions. Hence, Hydrogen Bomb where these reactions take place, is also called the Thermo Nuclear Device. On earth such conditions exist only in the fireball of an Atom Bomb.

The fuel in the Hydrogen bomb or the thermonuclear bomb is either the Hydrogen isotopes, Deuterium and Tritium (both are liquid gases and hence difficult to handle) or the solid precursor Lithium-6deuteride. This is why this bomb is also known as Tritium Boosted Nuclear Bomb. Since the required nuclear reaction can proceed only at the temperatures and pressures of the core of the Sun, the fuse of the Hydrogen Bomb is lit by a powerful (a 20 kiloton) Atom Bomb. Once the thermonuclear reactions are started, the extra energy they release can sustain the high temperature until much of the material is quickly 'burnt'.

The fuel for this bomb is very inexpensive and there is no limit to how much can be used in an individual Hydrogen bomb. So it can be shaped in smallest as well as biggest size, as the need may arise. Cost wise, a 20 Megaton Hydrogen bomb may be built at a cost of about 1 crore rupees.

Power of a Nuclear Bomb: The destructive power (yield) or the strength of a nuclear bomb is compared with the energy produced by a standard chemical explosive, Tri Nitro Toluene

(TNT). TNT is selected as a standard of explosive power because once it starts burning, it burns completely. The first fission (atomic) bomb test released the same energy as approximately 20,000 tons of TNT. Hence, we called it a 20 Kiloton bomb. The first thermonuclear (hydrogen) bomb test released the same amount of energy as approximately 10^6 tons of TNT. So, this was a One Megaton bomb. To have a feel of the explosiveness, we can see that one kiloton energy can convert 2 million liter of water into steam. Present day megaton bombs are about a million times more powerful than conventional TNT 'Blockbuster'.

Radio Activity: We mention these because in a nuclear explosion these rays are released in very large quantity. *Radio activity or Radio active decay is the set of various processes by which unstable atomic nuclei (nuclides) emit subatomic particles.* Heavy nuclei like Uranium, Radium etc., spontaneously keep on radiating certain invisible but harmful radiations. These radiations are of three types—*alpha, beta and gamma*.

Alpha particles radiate about 5MeV energy but can be easily stopped by even a thick sheet of paper. If they, somehow, enter our body, through dust or an open wound, they prove to be fatal.

Beta particles emit energy up to 5.6 MeV, but they can penetrate air through many feet. They can also penetrate through a few inches thick sheet of plastic or metal. If the body is exposed to them for a long time, beta radiations burn the skin, and it may prove to be fatal. To protect ourselves from these radiations, we need 2 to 10 inches thick wall of Lead or a three meter thick wall of concrete. Beta radiations cause cancer and inheritable disablement.

Gamma Radiations are high energy electromagnetic waves. The X-rays are actually another form of gamma rays.

Radioactive Lethal Dose: During an atomic explosion, the energy released is not only a million times worse but also each gram of Pu^{239} or U^{235} consumed must result in a gram of fission product which are initially radioactive. This is an extremely large amount of radioactivity and causes extremely serious and damaging biological effects.

If one gram of biological matter receives a radiation dose of 1 *rad* (a unit of radiation dose) then 100 ergs (unit of energy) of energy will be dissipated. A radiation dose of 400 rad is called a Lethal Dose. If a person receives 400 rad over his entire body in a short period of time, the biological damage is so great that there is about 50% chance for the individual to die.

Neutron Bomb: Neutron Bomb or Enhanced Radiation Weapon (ERW) is a small hydrogen bomb that produces minimal blast and heat but releases large amount of lethal radiations. The blast and heat effects delivered by this weapon are confined to an area only a few hundred meters in radius, but it throws off a massive wave of neutrons and gamma radiations, which can penetrate armor and several feet of earth. This radiation is extremely destructive to living tissue. Because of its short-range destructiveness and the absence of long range effect, the Neutron Bomb is an effective battlefield weapon. The Neutron Bomb would be highly effective against tanks and infantry formations on the battlefield but would not endanger concrete buildings in cities only a few miles away.

This battlefield weapon can be carried in a Lance-missile or delivered by a 200-millimetre howitzer, or possibly by attack aircraft. Actually, the neutron bomb has a theoretical deterrent effect. It discourages an armored ground assault by arousing the fear of neutron bomb counter attack. The bomb disables enemy tank crews in no time and those exposed would die within days.

The Neutron Bomb was conceived by Samuel T. Cohen in 1958 and testing was carried out in 1963 at Nevada test facility, America. Due to political reasons, the U.S. production of the bomb was postponed by President Jimmi Carter in 1978. But, President Ronald Reagan restarted production in 1981.

The U.S., Russia, France and China are understood to have tested ERW, although no country is currently known to deploy them. As for as India is concerned, its top nuclear scientists, K. Santhanam, Anil Kakodkar and Rajgopal Chidambaram has claimed that India is capable of fabricating a Neutron Bomb.

Santhanam says, "Though there are no immediate plans to produce the Neutron Bomb in view of various binding factors, sometime, somebody should tell us (the scientific community) we need a Neutron Bomb and we will make it." R. Chidambaram said that Indian nuclear scientists after the Pokhran-II tests can design and make nuclear weapons of any type and any size. The Neutron Bomb is essentially a low-yield thermonuclear device where the neutron production process dominates over the fission trigger. It is not difficult to build such a device. He also opined that India should develop pure-fusion Neutron Bomb that does not require fission.

Hydrodynamic Laws: Actual tests of nuclear explosives are not only to learn whether they perform as required, but also to gain from experimental discoveries. The design of fission and thermonuclear explosives requires a knowledge of the properties of materials at extremely high temperatures and pressures. An understanding of these properties, as well as the probabilities for various atomic and nuclear interactions, and the resulting hydrodynamic motions are obtained by a combination of theoretical calculations and experimental observations involving actual nuclear explosions. While the governing equations are generally known, their approximate solutions can usually be found only with the aid of very large and fast computers (Super Computers).

Computer Simulations: A Computer Simulation is a computer program or network of computers that attempts to simulate an abstract model of a particular system. Computer Simulations have become a useful part of mathematical modeling of many natural systems in computational physics, astrophysics, chemistry, biology, human systems in economics, psychology, social sciences and engineering. Simulations can be used to explore and gain new insights into new technology and to estimate the performance of systems too complex for analytical solutions.

Computer simulation was developed hand-in-hand with the rapid growth of the computer. It was first deployed on a large scale during the Manhattan Project in World-War-II to model the process of nuclear detonation. Computer simulation is often used as a substitution for modeling systems for which simple closed-form analytic solutions are not possible.

In the field of nuclear devices, the solutions of the complex equations along with data obtained from actual nuclear explosions and the knowledge of material properties at high pressures and temperatures are used to design nuclear weapons. The development of computer simulation techniques has made this job comparatively easier and cheaper. For this we need a specific data (the amount and form of energy, the values of heat, light and pressure produced, the speed of fission etc.) obtained from systematically performed experiments, as well as by theoretical calculations done with the help of a super computer. If we succeed to narrow down the difference between experimental and theoretical data to zero, we need not do the actual explosion for the nuclear test. That is, after achieving this systematic and minimum experimental data we can use simulation techniques to have new designs without actually performing the experimental tests. That is, we can design new types of nuclear bombs with different capabilities without actually testing them. Recently, US government has set up a Stockpile Stewardship Program. This will spend about $ 3 billion (Rupees 12,000 crore) for a National Ignition Facility lab where the condition of nuclear fusion can be replicated by laser energy. The US also has a super computer 1000 times faster than anything today for simulating nuclear tests. The US also has performed a sub-critical test where weapons and assemblies and even fissile material are tested in a way that there is no self-sustaining nuclear fission.

❑

2

The Energy and Power Problem

> ***"For a country like India, two measures of development are—Per Capita Electricity Consumption and Female Literacy and that these are better measures than the three parameters—per capita GNP, life expectancy at birth and adult literacy-used by the United Nations to define the Human Development Index."***
>
> ***—R. Chidambaram, addressing the Delhi University Convocation (20-3-2010).***

In the industrialised world, we use an enormous amount of energy as we go about our everyday lives. Energy and, in particular, electricity is now an essential part of society. Ambuj Sagar, a research associate at Harward's John F. Kennedy School writes, "The Planning Commission estimates that the total primary energy supply increased from 83 Million Tone Of Oil Equivalent (MTOE) in 1950-51 to 440 MTOE in 2001-02, commercial energy supply increased from 22 MTOE to about 300 MTOE, while power generation went up from 5 billion KWH (Kilo Watt Hour) to 515 billion KWH." The ability of petroleum producers to withhold the supply reveals the importance of energy independence and price.

Energy Situation In India: R. Chidambaram, a great nuclear scientist, while addressing the Delhi University (India) Convocation on March 20, 2010 said, *"For a country like India, two measures of development are Per Capita Electricity Consumption and Female Literacy and that these are better measures than the three parameters—per capita GNP, life expectancy at birth and adult literacy—used by the United Nations to define the Human Development Index.* Paul Maidment writes, "Over the last quarter of a century India's energy consumption has tripled. The rate of growth is faster than China, though the causes are the same: rapid economic development, a large and growing population and increasing urbanization. So is the potential threat to air quality and water supplies. Even under conservative estimates of growth, India's energy requirements are likely to increase by a further third in the second half of this decade, driven by industry, transportation and domestic electricity consumption, as living standards rise. Yet India's ambition to grow its economy at a long-term annual rate of 8% is running up against an energy constraint. Solving it will require continued reliance on fossile fuel—notably coal—greater energy imports and root-and-branch reform of electricity generation, which in India is an inadequate, insufficient and insolvent provision of power that is already causing environmental damage to water supplies."

India currently uses coal for about half of its energy needs. Few see that share changing much over the next two decades, even as over all energy use grows. The country risks creating the same environmental problems for itself that now confront China.

Now importing over 70% of her oil, India registered a trade deficit in 2004 for the first time in several years. A successful long-term energy strategy of India must emphacise next generation ways to use energy efficiency, and increase energy independence. India is too big and too late, as experts say, in the game to develop an oil-based energy economy, and she must leap-frog the industrial development model of the west. Lifting the huge Indian economy to higher economic standards will require creativity, vision, diplomacy and innovation.

More recently, the global warming is universally accepted as a serious problem which causes widespread melting of ice, noticeable climate changes and rising sea levels. This is due to the greenhouse gases,* mainly carbon dioxide, produced by burning fossile fuels such as petroleum, coal and natural gas. In the absence of an effective alternative fuel, the man is worried about rapidly exhausting these sources of energy and power generation. The world supply of gas and oil will be depleted in a few decades. The forests supplying fuel-wood are vanishing very rapidly. Even the supply of coal will last a few decades. So the man must confront the issue of developing clean and renewable energy sources in this century or face a climate disaster. Hoffert, an author, says, "*What our research clearly shows is that scientific innovation can only reverse this trend if we adopt an aggressive global strategy for developing alternative fuel sources that can produce up to three times the amount of power we use today.*"

Use of ***Ethanol*** is also no solution. Its production consumes nearly as much energy as it provides, and its use generates green house gas. *Solar power, wind power, the tidal power, hydroelectric power, hydrogen power, methane from buried*

---

* *Greenhouse effect is actually a good thing. It prevents incoming heat from the Sun from escaping strait back into space and keeps the global mean sur face temperature at around 15 degree Celsius. Without the green house effect, the Earth would be too cold for life to survive.* The ***problem*** we face is the ***Enhanced Green House Effect***. *The concentration of green house gases (mainly carbon dioxide) are building up in the atmosphere and this is preventing more heat from escaping, leading to an increase in the earth's temperature. This increased temperature is affecting ecosystems either directly by melting ice in arctic regions, which leads to loss of habitat for wildlife; indirectly by changing weather patterns, which can disrupt ecosystems which are used to certain climatic conditions. Some areas will see significant changes such as sea-level rise, more extreme weather events and the spread of diseases such as malaria.*"

organic material, the energy from waste and other renewable power sources such as the earth's internal heat or gravitational energy, are advocated by some,* but so far, no solution has been proposed that would be both affordable and complete.

A study shows that currently world's power consumption is about 12 trillion Watt, 85% of it is produced from fossile fuels. To stabilise the amount of carbon dioxide emitted to the atmosphere by the middle of the century while still permitting the current level of global economic expansion would require production of about 30 trillion Watt of power worldwide using power systems that do not emit carbon dioxide.

Energy from Nuclear Fission: Experts say that none of the known alternate energy source is technically ready to take the place of fossile fuels. *But an alternative* ***clean and renew able energy source is Nuclear Fission.*** **The fission of Uranium, Plutonium or Thorium, generates heat, which is used to heat water to produce steam.** The steam drives turbines which turn generators

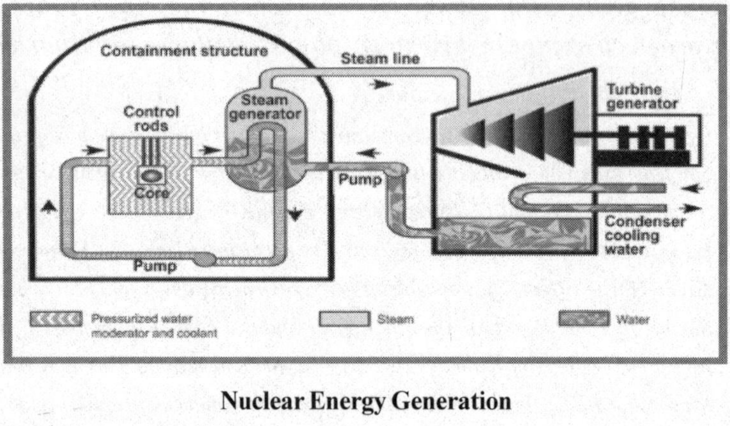

Nuclear Energy Generation

* *renewable energy is energy that is constantly renewed and will never run out. Similarly, non renewable energy sources are sources that are finite and that will deplete as they are used, eventually running out altogether.*

to produce electricity. The world scientists have successfully tried to control the nuclear chain reaction and use this as a source of energy. The technological achievement of controlling the nuclear fission by pioneers like H.J. Bhabha and others have made possible the peaceful use of fission in the form of *nuclear reactors*, which in turn are used for power generation. Even this is not a final answer because of the limited Uranium deposits available on earth. The fission reactors have only extended the energy problem to few centuries, as Uranium deposits on the earth will exhaust in few centuries at the most. According to an estimate the Uranium resources would last for less than 30 years if nuclear fission was used to make 10 trillion watt of power per year.

But the use of Nuclear Energy is not safe. The reasons are:

Nuclear Power Plant

(1) Accidents such as Chernobyl (Russia) in 1986, and Fukushima (Japan) in March, 2011, at nuclear power stations could result in the release of vast amounts of highly radioactive material into the atmosphere. While the chances of such accidents are low, the impact can be very high.

(2) Dealing with spent nuclear fuel is as problematic as green house gases. Nuclear waste can stay dangerously radioactive for thousands of years, and there is still no solution for dealing with it safely.

(3) There is also a risk of proliferation of the nuclear material. Nuclear waste can be used to make nuclear weapons, and nuclear power stations would be prime targets for terrorists.

Electricity from Sunlight: Most sources of renewable energy come either directly or indirectly from the Sun, although there are other sources such as the Earth's internal heat source or gravitation energy. Though expensive to build, the system which abandons fossil fuel and should be cheap to operate, is the electricity from Sunlight which has no operating cost. All the energy that the earth has stored and almost all the energy it receives every day comes from the Sun. About 89,000 terawatt (1TW=a million million (quadrillion) watt) falls on the earth, while total usage (in 2004) was only 15 TW, of which 87% was provided by fossil fuels. If we were to get most of our usable energy from the Sun, we would solve many of the most important problems, including the price and availabilty of petroleum as well as the noxious by-products associated with using nuclear power and fossil fuels. Relying on the Sun rather than petroleum would also permit us to be much less involved with events in the middle-east. But to meet the current needs, US alone would require *Sun Collectors* covering 1000 square miles.

To obtain *solar power through satellites*, we would need nearly 650 orbiting solar arrays which will make electricity, convert it to microwaves and then, beam it towards ground antennas where it would be converted back to electricity.

Wind Power: Windmills have been used for centuries for grinding grain or for pumping water. Wind turbines are made up of a rotor, which usually has three blades, and this is mounted on the top of a high tower in order to catch the faster wind. The rotor generates electricity. It should be mentioned that wind turbines are noisy, unsightly and a danger to wild life.

Wind Farm

Hydrogen Fuel Cells: Gaseous hydrogen and air are fed in a hydrogen fuel cell. The H-gas atoms get split into protons and electrons by a catalyst, and the protons travel through a membrane which prevents the electrons from getting through. This forces the electrons to find another way of getting back to the protons, and this via a wire. When electrons travel through the wire they produce an electric current which can be used to power vehicles or to run house-hold appliances.

But the separation of H-atoms from water by electrolysis requires an input of more electricity than is actually received from the gaseous hydrogen.

Tidal Energy: A huge dam (barrage) is built across a bay or an estuary where there is a large difference in water levels between high and low tides. The high tide will bring a vast amount of water into the bay, before gates are closed when the water level is at its highest to prevent the water from leaving when the tide goes back. The water stored behind the dam is then released through holes at the bottom of the dam at highest speed. The rushing water drives the turbines which generates electricity. The process is repeated again and again with every change in tide. But tidal energy systems are very expensive to build.

Hydroelectric Power: Hydroelectric power stations exploit the huge gravitational (potential) energy that is contained in rivers in mountaneous regions. A very high dam is constructed to trap water in a river valley and allow a huge increase in water level. The water is then flown through the holes at the bottom containing turbines. When the water flows through the pipes at high pressure it turns turbines which generates electricity.

The construction of hydroelectric plants is very costly and leads to the displacement of many reparian communities, and causes devastating effects on ecosystem's either side of the dam.

Geothermal Power: The centre of the earth is extremely hot, around 6,000 degrees Celsius. This heat drives the movement of the earth's tectonic plates which causes earthquakes and volcanic eruptions. It is generally believed that the temperature increases by 1 degree Celsius for every 36 meters descended. This renewable energy source exploits the energy stored in the rocks under the earth's surface. Holes are drilled down to the hot rocks in order to release the steam formed due to the heat in the rocks. The steam is used to drive turbines, which turn generators and produce electricity. It should be noted that some hazardous gases may come up from the rocks, and their handling and disposal may be a problem.

Energy from Nuclear Fusion: If like fission, the fusion process could be used for energy production, it would be about six times more efficient than fission of Uranium. Scientists from all over the world were startled when Professor Homi Jehangir Bhabha, head of India's Atomic Energy Commission and president of 'UN International Conference on the Peaceful Uses of Atomic Energy' held in Geneva in August, 1955 made the following statement:

"When we learn how to liberate fusion energy in a controlled manner, the energy problems of the world will truly have been solved for ever, for the fuel will be as potential as the heavy water (Deuterium Oxide) in the ocean."

A limitless supply of energy for mankind was being predicted by a first rate nuclear physicist. Even men who could see undreamed of developments in this exploding field of nuclear energy, rubbed their eyes and searched for clues and shreds of information on which this almost unbelievable prediction was made. There is an unlimited and inexpensive supply of Deuterium in the water of the lakes and oceans, which is not so in case of other fuels. A large amount of effort, since then, has gone into solving this technological problem of controlling the fusion, but we have achieved little success so far.

Efforts to Control Fusion: Total amount of deuterium in world's seas and oceans is estimated to be of the order of 10^5 tones which, if utilized by fusion reaction, would be enough to fulfil the world's power requirements for millions of years to come. Many ways are suggested to achieve a controlled fusion:

1. Fusion from *Plasma:* *Plasma is actually a highly ionized gas comprised of free electrons and positive ions.*

Scientists are trying to obtain energy through nuclear fusion by heating Deuterium present in sea water (1 part in 5000) at 10^7degree Kelvin. When mixture of Deuterium and Tritium is heated up to 10^7degree Kelvin, the fusion will start in the neighbouring nuclei. In this process one Deuterium nucleus and one Tritium nucleus are fused to produce one helium nucleus and one neutron accompanied by 17.6 Mev of energy.

$$ {}_1H^2 + {}_1H^3 \longrightarrow {}_2He^4 + {}_0n^1 + 17.6 \text{ Mev} $$

So this process can become an unlimited source of energy.

Tokamak

Russian physicist Igor Tamm and Andrei Sakharov have made a fusion reactor device known as Tokamak in 1950s. It is a hollow stainless steel toroid of the shape of cycle tube, which is wrapped with the coil of a thick copper wire. When a heavy current is passed through this coil, a magnetic field is produced in Tokamak.

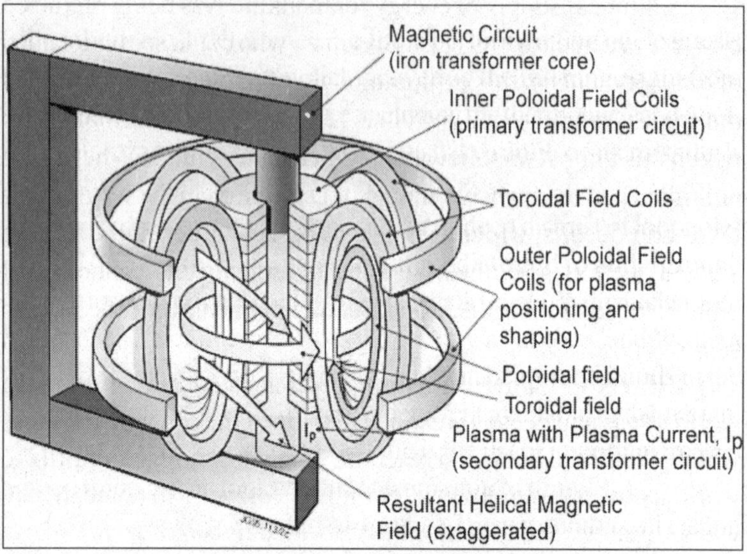

A Tokamak Design of Fusion Reactor

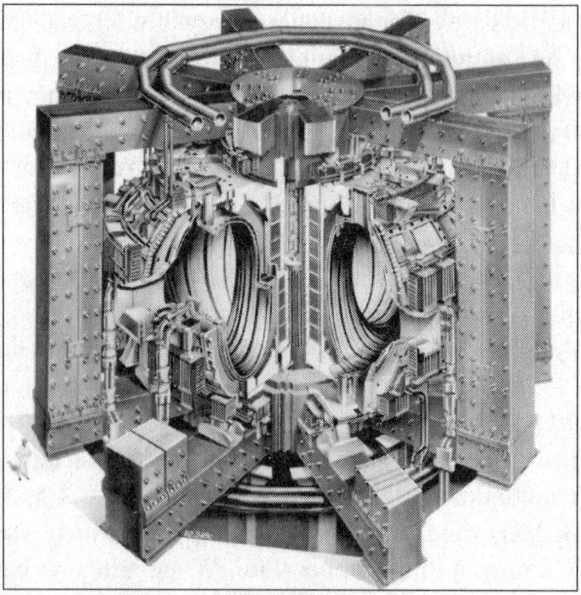

The Tokamak

The toroid is filled with a mixture of Deuterium and Tritium which is turned into plasma due to the discharge process. A current of 10^6 Ampere is flown through the plasma by transformer action, which heats the plasma to 10^7 degree Kelvin and produces a magnetic field which does not allow the hot electrons and ions to disperse. Plasma temperature is raised to 10^8 degree Kelvin by making use of neutral beam, microwaves or radio waves. At this temperature fusion occurs. Each fusion reaction results in the production of an alpha particle and a neutron, as shown in the above *nuclear equation*. The neutrons carry most of the energy and can escape the confining fields. They are captured in the walls of the Tokamak where they generate heat. A coolant circulating through the walls is passed through an heat exchanger to produce the steam to drive turbines, as in a conventional power station. The walls also double as a 'breeding blanket' in which neutrons react with Lithium to produce further Tritium.

The Tokamak is one of several types of magnetic confinement devices, and is one of the most-researched candidates for producing *thermo nuclear fusion power.* Magnetic fields are used for confinement since no solid material could withstand the extremely high temperature of the plasma. *An alternative to the Tokamak is the* ***Stellarator***.

After initial efforts by Russia, America, Japan, Germany, France and England, India also started working on Tokamak.

2. Fusion Induced by Laser: Quite intense laser rays are thrown on one cm diameter sphere of solid Deuterium Tritium from all sides. These lasers convert the sphere into plasma in a moment and heat its outer part so much that the inner part is squeezed due to pressure and afterward gets heated also.

A lot of progress has been made in this direction. In India the work is going on in this field at BARC and CAT India.

3. Fusion from a Pulsed Power Source: In April, 2003 scientists from Sandia National Laboratories reported achieving fusion with a blast of X–rays compressing a capsule of hydrogen to conditions approaching those at the centre of the Sun. Such controlled explosions would not be large enough to be dangerous and might offer an alternative way of generating electricity by harnessing fusion.

Jeff Quintenz, director of the Pulsed Power Sciences Centre at Sandia, likened the approach to burning coal in a furnace. It is something more like an internal combustion Engine, in which power is generated through a series of explosions. But decades of research and expensive reactors are needed before a commercial power plant is possible.

❑

3

Weapon of Mass Destruction (WMD)

> ***"Through the work of Juliot in France as well as Fermi and Szilard in America, it may become possible to set up a nuclear chain reaction in a large mass of Uranium, by which vast amount of power and large quantities of new radium-like elements would be generated……and it is conceivable that extremely powerful bomb of a new type may thus be constructed. A single bomb of this type, carried by boat, and exploded in a port, might very well destroy the whole port together with some of the surrounding territory……"1***
>
> ***—'Letter of Conscience' from Albert Einstein to President Franklin D. Roosevelt (August 2, 1939.)***

Perhaps no common man has seen an Atom Bomb. But a mere name when heard, brings before the eyes—A monster of a mushroom type tree of nuclear dust growing from a fire ball and swallowing every thing living and destroying every symbol of civilization on a large area on the earth. Everybody, though horrified, has a curiosity to know about this weapon of mass destruction.

History: In January 1934, Enrico Fermi along with his group of scientists in Rome, started the study of artificial radioactivity by bombarding different substances with neutrons. In May 1934, the team bombarded Uranium also, but they could not understand the results. Had Fermi completely understood these results, the whole world, including Hitler in Germany, would have known back in 1934 about the possibility of an atomic bomb.

Fermi was a Roman Catholic but married to a Jew. Antisemetic laws against Jews were imported from Germany into Italy where Fermi was born. The Fermi family was, therefore, not feeling comfortable in fascist Italy. Fermi was awarded the Noble Prize for his discovery and production of new isotopes. In December 1938, when Fermi reached Sweden along with his family (as it was a custom for one's family to accompany the prize winner) to receive his prize, he, instead of going back to Italy after receiving the prize, managed to fly to United State and get his family out of fascist Italy.

Enrico Fermi

Meanwhile, American President Franklin D. Roosevelt sent some manuscripts of scientific papers by E. Fermi and L. Szilard to Albert Einstein and asked for his expert opinion. Einstein wrote back on August 2, 1939, in what is known as 'Letter of Conscience', "*Through the works of Juliot in France as well as Fermi and Szilard in America, it may become possible to set up a nuclear chain reaction in a large mass of Uranium, by which vast amount of power and large quantities of new radium-like elements would be generated……and it is conceivable that extremely powerful bomb of a new type may thus be constructed. A large bomb of this type, carried by boat, and exploded in a port, might very well destroy the whole port together with some of the surrounding territory....* ".

Under the shadow of Second World War when Americans were craving desperately for a horrible destructive weapon, a team in Germany headed by Otto Hahn and including Strassman and Miss Lise Meitner actually succeeded in splitting Uranium atom by neutron bullets into two halves, three neutrons and enormous amount of energy. Incidentally, the Kaiser Wilhelm Institute in Berlin-Dehlem where this experiment was conducted was located only a few kilometers away from Hitler's Chancellery. Fortunately for Allies, the significance of this tremendous release of energy again did not attract much attention of these scientists in the beginning. That was because the leader of the team, a chemist, was interested only in chemical change that had occurred. Miss Meitner being a physicist, concentrated on the release of energy and was convinced that tremendous energy trapped in Uranium atom awaited uncorking and use by mankind. But she would never let Hitler know about it. She was a pious and god-fearing Jew. She was convinced that Hitler will use this great source of energy in destroying thousands of human lives and she would have to bear the sin of all these killings. To her relief (!) despite her distinguished position as head of the physics department, she was marked by the Nazis for arrest and concentrated camp; knowing this she fled to Stockholm. Here she met Robert O. Frisch, another German Jew refugee scientist attached to Neils Bohr laboratory. It was here, Meitner and Frisch gave the name 'Nuclear Fission' to this phenomenon of split in Uranium nucleus. The two sent all the details of the fission to Bohr who was then in America. Bohr shared this new development with Fermi, the original worker in this field.

Lise Meitner

With the 1938 discovery of nuclear fission Germany ministry of munitions entrusted the job of developing use of nuclear fission in warfare to a team of scientists which included Otto Hahn and Geiger (Inventor of Geiger Counter—an instrument to detect radioactive emissions). Germany, in this field, had a two year head-start on developing nuclear energy. Germany also had in its grasp two materials critical to its development—heavy water and Uranium. They were available in abundance in Norway and Czechoslovakia, both under Nazi control. This alarmed the refugee scientists in USA. American fear was that the Nazis would shape it into a WMD (Weapon of Mass Destruction). President Roosevelt who had already received Einstein report on nuclear fission, created an advisory committee on Uranium which popularly came to be known as Manhattan Project.

The formulas for refining Uranium and putting together a working atomic bomb were created and seen to their logical ends by some of the greatest minds of that time. Chief among the people who unlashed the power of the atom was Robert Oppenheimer, who oversaw the project from conception to completion. The project involved teams of scientists at several locations throughout the United States, each working on a separate problem connected with the task of designing and building the Atom Bomb.

Fermi team succeeded in completing a self-sustaining nuclear chain reaction. In 1940's visitors to Chicago University could see a bronze plaque mounted outside its squash court which read, "*On December 2, 1942, man achieved here the first self-sustaining chain reaction and thereby initiated the controlled release of nuclear energy*." Fermi ultimately, received the due credit of completing nuclear chain reaction, which had slipped from his hands earlier. But the bomb was still away.

Though, it took two and a half years to test the first ever nuclear bomb, yet the game of deterring the enemy with a nuclear attack started much earlier. British files released on December 1, 2002, reveal plans to threaten Germany with a nuclear bomb during World War-II to prevent Hitler launching V2 rockets at London. In the summer of 1944, Britain tried to bluff the Nazis out of using the supersonic V2 rockets. But the bluff failed. Hitler proved to be smarter. Less than two weeks after the threat, V2s began raining on Britain. In the last seven months of war over 3000 V2s were launched, killing some 2700 people.

The Trinity Explosion (The first Atomic Bomb Detonation): At a laboratory at Los Alamos, the efforts to obtain fissionable isotopes, coupled with design efforts, resulted in a bomb. At 5:30 AM on July 16, 1945, white blaze that stretched from the basin of the Jemez Mountains in North New Mexico to the still dark skies, turned orange as the atomic fire ball began shooting upwards at 360 feet per second, reddening and pulsing as it cooled. The characteristic mushroom cloud of radioactive vapour materialized at 30 thousand feet beneath the cloud, all that remained of the soil at the blast site were fragments of jade green radioactive glass created by the heat of the reaction.

What a terrifying scene it was! The brilliant light from the detonation pierced the early morning skies with such intensity that residents from a faraway neighboring community would swear that the Sun came up twice that day. Even more astonishing is that a blind girl saw the flash 120 miles away. Upon witnessing the explosion, its creators had mixed reactions:

Isidor Rabi felt that equilibrium in nature had been upset as if humankind had become a threat to the world it inhabited.

The test director, Ken Bainbridge told Oppenheimer, "Now we are all sons of bitches."

Robert Oppenheimer himself, though ecstatic about the success of the project, boasted quoting a remembered fragment from the Bhagvat Gita, " *Now I have become death, the destroyer of the worlds.*" That is

Robert Oppenheimer

कालोऽस्मि लोकक्षय कृत्प्रवृद्धो
लोकान्समाहर्तुमिहप्रवृत्तः ।

(Gita 11/32)

(I am Death—the destroyer of worlds. This time I am indulged in destroying the worlds).

Mass Destruction in Japan by Little Boy: Less than one month later, on August 6, 1945 at 8:16 AM, a 12.5 kiloton Uranium bomb was dropped on Hiroshima. The bomb, 3.2 meter long, 0.73 meter round and 4080 kilogram in weight was ironically nicknamed 'Little Boy'. The Aioi Bridge, one of 81 bridges connecting the seven branched delta of the Ota River, was the target. The bomb was air-dropped from a B-29 Super fortress 'Enola Gay'. It missed the target by only 800 feet. *In an instant, 66,000 people were killed and 69,000 injured by the Explosion. The area of total vaporization from the atomic bomb blast, measured one half mile in diameter; total destruction one mile in diameter; severe blast damage as much as two miles in diameter. Within a diameter of two and a half miles, everything flammable burnt. The remaining area of the zone was riddled with serious blazes that stretched out to the final edge at a little over three miles in diameter.*

Now the Fat Man: Three days later on August 9, 1945, another Japanese big city, Nagasaki, fell to the same treatment. This time a 22 kiloton Plutonium bomb, nicknamed 'Fat Man' (3.25 meter long.1.52 meter round and 4206 kilogram in weight) was dropped on the city. Though Fat Man missed its target by over a mile and a half, it still leveled nearly half the city with a population of 4,22,000. In a split second 39,000 people died and over 25,000 were injured.

Physicists who have studied these two atomic explosions estimate that the bombs utilized only 1/10th of I percent of their respective explosive capabilities.

The destructive ability of atom bomb does not stop here. Atom bomb fallout creates another hazard as well. The rain that follows any atomic detonation is laden with radioactive particles, and many survivors of the Hiroshima and Nagasaki blasts succumbed to radio poisoning. The Atomic Bomb detonation also has the hidden lethal surprise of affecting future generations of those who live through it. Leukemia is among the greatest of affections that are passed on to the offspring of survivors.

While high altitude atomic detonations are hardly lethal, one small, high-altitude detonation can deliver a serious enough EMP (Electro-Magnetic Pulse) to scramble all things electronics, from copper wires to computer's CPU, within a 50 mile radius.

The hunger for deadly weapons was not pacified yet. Efforts continued to build a much deadlier weapon, called Hydrogen Bomb. United States successfully tested the 10.4 Megaton Hydrogen bomb on November 1, 1952. Later, America developed the Neutron Bomb also.

Types of Nuclear Weapons: In a nuclear weapon, the efficiency of an atomic explosion depends not only upon the adequate supercritical assembly of the enriched fuel but also on the sophistication of the technique which ensures that a significant fraction of the fuel is consumed before the weapon destroys itself. To get the maximum yield, the nuclear reaction should be 'ignited' in such a way that the fuel 'combustion' should be complete. That is 100% fuel should be 'burned'. So there are two techniques giving two types of Nuclear Bombs.

Fission Bomb (also called Atom Bomb): We know that nuclear chain reaction is a mass-reaction, any technique that we adopt to detonate a fission bomb should manage the fuel assembly to be supercritical. As we have discussed earlier, there are two methods to start an exponentially growing nuclear chain reaction. One way is to bring two sub-critical masses together so that the combined mass becomes supercritical. The second approach is to compress a sub-critical mass of the fuel so much that its increased density does not allow the neutrons to escape from it. That is, the mass becomes supercritical. Hence, ***there are two mechanisms to detonate the atom bomb***.

1. ***Gun-type Assembly Method:*** In this simplest and classical method a mass of fissile material is assembled into a sub critical mass and fired with a projectile made of sub critical mass of the same material so that the two are held together into a supercritical assembly. In other words, the critical mass of nuclear fuel is divided keeping the components separate. At the time of explosion, these components are propelled together cataclysmically by a high explosive gun. The Hiroshima bomb was a gun-assembly. The fuel was enriched Uranium.

This technique is unsuitable to a Plutonium bomb for which we use another technique called implosion. Platinum is considered impractical for gun method because of early triggering due to Pu^{240} contamination and due to its time constant for prompt critical fission being much shorter than that of U^{235}.

2. ***Implosion Assembly Meth d:*** It is a complex, sophisticated but modern technique. It uses a single core of fissile material of lower than critical mass placed at the centre of spherical weapon. The outer part of the sphere consists of a layer of closely fitted and specially shaped devices called lenses. These lenses consist of conventional high explosive and are designed to concentrate the blast towards the center of the spherical bomb. Each segment of the high explosive is provided with a detonator, which in turn is wired to all other segments. An electrical impulse explodes all the chunks of the high explosives simultaneously, resulting in a detonation wave that converges radially towards the centre of the weapon. This inward traveling blast wave causes the core to implode and hence name of the technique is implosion method. As it collapses in on itself its density increases up to three times and a supercritical fuel assembly is produced. A trigger sends a beam of neutrons that causes a chain reaction fissioning the Plutonium nuclei. Thereafter the bomb explodes. The Trinity test bomb and Nagasaki bomb were of implosion type. The fuel used was obviously P^{239}.

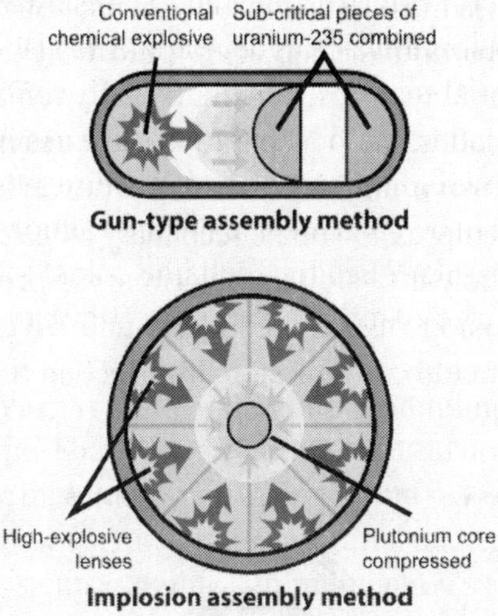

(Explosion Techniques)

It should be noted that such implosion devices require precision machining which can be achieved after collecting the adequate sophisticated data from a large number of tests.

Thermonuclear Weapon (Hydrogen Bomb): The second basic type of nuclear weapon is Hydrogen Bomb, which produces a large amount of energy through nuclear fusion reaction. However, all such weapons derive a significant portion (sometimes a majority) of their energy from fission (including fission induced by neutrons from fusion reactions). Unlike fission weapons, there are no inherent limits on the energy released by thermonuclear weapons.

The most popular design of Hydrogen Bomb called *Teller-Ulam Thermonuclear Bomb* is described in the Figure below. This was the device tested originally at Bikini. This design accounts for all multi-megaton yield Hydrogen Bombs. Its design concept is used in most of the world's nuclear weapons. It is referred to as 'the secret of the Hydrogen Bomb' because it employs hydrogen fusion to generate neutrons, though in most applications the bulk of its destructive energy comes from *uranium fission, not hydrogen fusion*.

It is named for Edward Teller and Stanislaw Ulam who were the chief contributors towards its development in 1951 for the United States. Its essential features, which officially remained secret for nearly three decades, are (i) separation of stages into a triggering 'primary' explosive and a much more powerful 'secondary' explosive, (ii) compression of the secondary by gamma and X-rays coming from nuclear fission in the primary, a process called the radiation implosion of the secondary, and (iii) heating of the secondary, after cold compression, by a second fission explosion

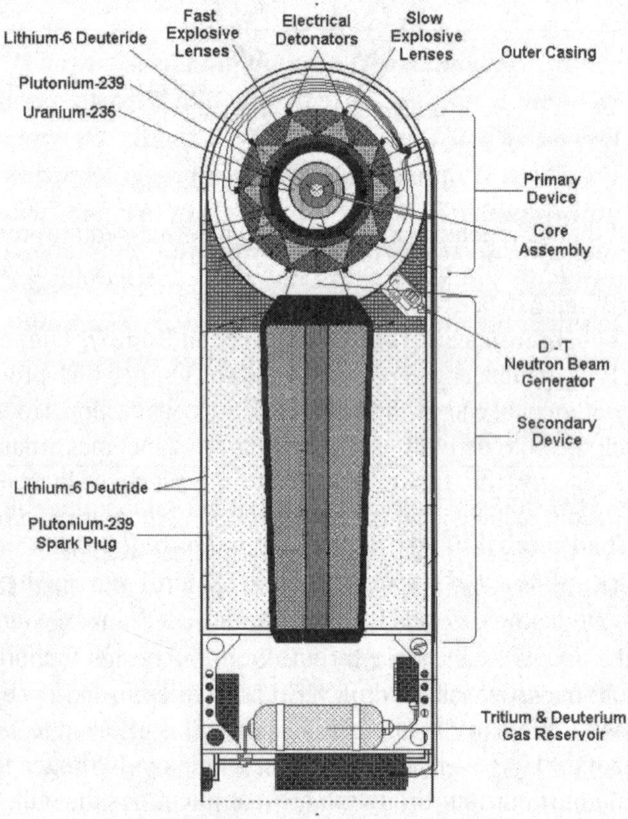

Teller-Ulam Thermonuclear Bomb

inside the secondary. In simple words, it uses the energy of a fission bomb to compress and heat fusion fuel. This is accomplished by placing a fission bomb and fusion fuel (Tritium, Deuterium or Lithium Deuteride) in proximity within a special, radiating–reflecting container. When the fission bomb is detonated, gamma and X-rays emitted first compress the fusion fuel, then heat it to thermonuclear temperature. The ensuing fusion reaction creates enormous numbers of high-speed neutrons, which can then induce fission in materials not normally prone to it, such as depleted Uranium. Each of these components is known as a 'stage', with the fission bomb as the 'primary' and the fusion capsule as the 'secondary'. In large hydrogen bombs, about half of the yield, and much of the resulting nuclear fallout, comes from the final fission of depleted Uranium. Fusion products are typically non-radioactive.

Depleted Uranium is considered a weapon of mass destruction and is banned for use in warfare by International Law. Yet United States and Israel have used it many times. The U.S. military has used thousands of tons of depleted Uranium in Yugoslavia, Afghanistan, Kuwait and Iraq, sickening tens of thousands of civilians and its own soldiers. Depleted Uranium contaminates air, water, food and land for ever. It is the ultimate 'Dirty Bomb'.

The ***Radiation Implosion*** mechanism, mentioned above, is a *heat engine* exploiting the temperature difference between the hot radiation channel, surrounding the secondary, and the relatively cool interior of the secondary. This temperature difference is briefly maintained by a massive heat barrier called *pulsar*'. The pulsar is also an implosion temper, increasing and prolonging the compression of the secondary, and, if made of Uranium, which it usually is, it undergoes fission by capturing the neutrons produced by fusion. In most Teller-Ulam weapons, fission of the pulsar dominates the explosion and produces *radio-active fission product fallout*.

The first test of this principle was conducted by the United States in 1952, although it does not count as a 'bomb'. The first actual Hydrogen bomb was detonated by the Soviet Union on August

12, 1953. It was called the RDS-6s 'Sloika' and it gained the nickname 'Joe 4' in the U.S. In the Soviet Union, the Teller-Ulam design was known as Andraei Sakharov's '*third idea*', the first tested in 1955 in an actual bomb RDS-6s 'Truba'.

By chaining together numerous stages with increasing amounts of fusion fuel, thermonuclear bombs can be made to an almost arbitrary yield, the largest ever detonated (the Tsar Bomba of USSR) was of 50 Megaton. Most thermonuclear weapons are considerably smaller than this, due to practical constraints arising from the space and weight requirements of missile warheads.

A hydrogen bomb is considered to be comparatively safe, as it librates less amount of dangerous radiations. But generally hydrogen bomb is covered with a layer of U^{238}. The neutrons which escape from the chain reaction, attack this layer. As a result U^{238} nuclei get fissionesd and emit energy like an Atom Bomb. Thus a single bomb works as hydrogen bomb as well as Atom Bomb. Such bombs are extremely dangerous.

Because of the facility to miniaturize the hydrogen bomb, these can also be used in missiles. Apart from this, the small bombs to be launched from submarines and air planes are also hydrogen bombs. The small nuclear bombs are very useful in achieving highest technique required in nuclear and space fields.

If the shield of the hydrogen bomb is made from a non-fissionable material, we get what is known as *Low Yield Bomb*. The impact of such low yield bombs is limited to a small area of the enemy's army or a pointed target like enemy's nuclear arsenal centre. Hence they can be used with less hesitation.

It seems India has tried to verify this capability through its may1998 tests.

It is believed that America has 250 ton W-54 low yield bombs which can be taken anywhere by soldiers on their back. The technique to make such bombs is with the US and Russia only, and probably India has become the third such country who has developed this technique.

Dirty Bomb: Actually, the Dirty Bomb is a speculative radiological weapon. It is a conventional explosive combined with radioactive material. The purpose of this weapon is to contaminate area around the explosion with radioactive material, hence we call it *Dirty*. Though such a Radiological Dispersal Device (RDD) would be designed to disperse radioactive material over a large area, a conventional explosive device would likely have more lethal effect than the radioactive material. Calculations on a test explosion, done by the United States Department of Energy, show that even if everyone stays in the affected area for one year, the radiation exposure would be fairly high but not fatal. Analysis of the nuclear fallout from the Chernobyl disaster confirms this, showing that the effect on many people in the surrounding area, although not those in close proximity, was almost negligible. The purpose of the dirty bomb is not to cause many deaths but to create psychological harm through mass panic, terror and ignorance. For this reason dirty bombs are not the '*weapon of mass destruction', but a 'weapon of mass disruption'*. Several analysits have predicted that RDD will neither sicken nor kill many people. According to majority of people involved in an RDD incidence, the radiation health risks are small as comparable to the health risk from smoking five packets of cigarettes on a daily basis. Statements from the U.S. Government after 9/11 may have contributed unnecessarily to the public fear of a dirty bomb.

Since the 9/11 attacks the fear of terrorist groups using dirty bombs has increased. There have only ever been two cases of Caesium-containing bombs, both involved Chechan separatists, and neither was detonated. The first attempt was carried out in November, 1955, when a Caesium-137 source wrapped in explosives was found burried in Moscow, which amounted to only a publicity stunt. The second attempt was in December, 1998, when a container was found fitted with radioactive material attached to an explosive mine.

Boosted Fission Bomb: A boosted fission weapon is a fission bomb which increases its explosive yield through a small amount of fusion reaction, but it is not a fusion bomb. In the boosted bomb, the neutrons produced by the fusion reaction serve primarily to increase the efficiency of the fission bomb. It is important to note that the use of a few grams of a mixture of deuterium and tritium, can boost the yield of a fission bomb by 5 to 10 times. So we can make a boosted fission device by using deuterium and tritium. This also reduces the size of the bomb.

Special Purpose Bombs: A Neutron Bomb is a thermonuclear weapon specially designed for the purpose of relatively small explosive yield but a relatively large amount of neutron radiations.

A weapon known as ***Salted Bomb*** is obtained by surrounding a nuclear weapon with suitable materials (such as Cobalt or Gold). This device can produce exceptionally large quantities of Radioactive contaminations.

The Mushroom Cloud: From physics point of view, the explosion would be somewhat spherical in space. Nuclear weapons are usually detonated above the ground (not upon impact, because most of the energy would be dispelled into the ground) in order to maximize the effect of their spherical expanding fireball and the blow wave. After immediate detonation, the fire ball itself begins to rise into the air, acting on the same principle as a hot air balloon.

What a distant onlooker observes during a nuclear blast? He sees a dazzling flash, a complete dark and then another flash in succession. When he comes out of this spell and adjusts his eyes, he finds a monstrously towering cloud in the sky. The scientific explanation of this phenomenon is as follows.

On detonation, the bomb turns into a rapidly expanding fire ball. The exploding core emits soft X-rays, which ionize the surrounding air, making it transparent to light. The fire ball becomes so bright as if more than thousands of Suns are put together. This reminds us the description of the dazzling brightness of Vishwaroop shown by Lord Krishna to Arjun when He says:

Mushroom Cloud

दिवि सूर्य सहस्त्रस्य भवेद्युगपदुत्थित।
यदि भाः सदृशी सा स्याद्भासस्तस्य महात्मनः॥

Gita (11/12)

(Even the light from thousands of Suns shining together may not mach His light.)

Then the core begins to cool. X-radiations slow down to be replaced by the ultraviolet rays, visible light and by infrared rays. The speed of the shock wave-front slows down to the speed of sound, and turns incandescent. The light cannot penetrate the air superheated by the shock wave and therefore, the explosion vanishes for some time to be seen again when the temperature starts falling. *The 'double flash' is the final confirmation of a nuclear blast*. The mushroom cloud of nuclear blast is seen last of all when the radiation has fallen sufficiently for vaporized and radioactive dirt sucked up by the explosion to become visible.

Disaster Created by Nuclear Blast: A common man does not have the idea of gravity of disaster which this WMD can create. Initially even the scientists could not have the exact estimate of the explosive power of these bombs. According to news in 1954, about the making and experimenting of the hydrogen bomb by Russia and America, the explosion of the American bomb was so powerful that even the instruments made to measure its strength were smashed. A pathetic description of the effects of the nuclear blast is given in a paper by Karl Z. Morgan:

The first thing that victims experience is the intense flux of photons (light) from the blast. This releases 70 to 80 per cent of the bomb's energy. The effects go up to third degree thermal burns, and these are the causes of the initial deaths.

The next phenomenon is the *supersonic blast front*, which is seen before it is heard. (This is because light travels much faster than sound as we see in case of flash and sound due to lightening). The pressure front has the effect of blowing away anything in its path. In Hiroshima and Nagasaki, heavy steel girders were found bent at right angles by this supersonic pressure.

Next is the *overpressure phase*. It would feel like being a few hundred meters under water. To have a feel of this pressure, we should know that at a few thousand meters under the sea, pressurized hulls implode. Gradually, pressure dies off and there is a negative overpressure phase, with a reversed blast wind. This reversal is due to air rushing back to fill the void left by the explosion.

When air gradually returns to room temperature, fire caused by electrical destruction and ignited debris, turns the place into a fire storm. It is estimated that over 50,000 people died in the first few days of the Hiroshima bombing.

Those who, somehow, survive this holocaust suffer most. It is probably better not to survive a nuclear blast. While radioactivity produced due to blast kills immediately at high levels, it causes extreme diseases and suffering at comparatively lower but persistent levels. Other fallout is that radioactive particles will be carried as radioactive dust and will impregnate soil, air and water for few years to come. Even the children born by parents who inhale the radioactive dust will be infected by those extreme diseases. Same is with other animals if they eat grass on the infected soil. The vagaries of the weather means that radioactivity is carried not only to area surrounding the intended targets, but even to the neighbouring countries.

Keeping in view the extent and type of the damage a nuclear explosion can do, the whole affected area, according to Karl Z. Morgan, can be divided into five concentric circular zones. The radius of each area depends upon the bomb type as given in the following Table 3.1.

1. *Vaporization Point:* At ground zero—graphically termed the vaporization point—everything in the area is vaporized by the atomic blast. The fatality rate is 98 per cent. But two out of hundred people who survive have only temporary reprieve. They will die in a matter of hours, if not in minutes, of shock and flash radiation burns. The wind velocity is 512 kilometers per hour (kmph), enough to flatten a city of high rises into a level plane. The overpressure is mind-blowing, 25 pounds per square inch (psi). This is a pressure sufficient to inflate a truck tier.

2. *Total Destruction Zone:* In next concentric circular zone, total destruction occurs in the area. All the structures above ground are destroyed and the fatality rate is 90 per cent. The over-pressure is still very high, 17 psi and the winds move at 464 kmph.

3. *Severe Blast Damage Zone:* All factories and other large scale buildings in this area collapse. There is severe damage to highway bridges. Rivers sometimes flow countercurrent. Fatalities are 65%, while other 30% are severely injured. The overpressure is down to 9psi while the wind velocity is 416 kmph.

Table 3.1. Blast Zone Radii for Three Different Bomb Types

Blast Zone	*10 Kiloton*	*1 Megaton*	*20 Megaton*
1. Vaporization point	0.50 mile	2.50 miles	8.75 miles
2. Total Destruction	1.00 mile	3.75 miles	14.0 miles
3. Severe Blast damage	1.75 miles	6.50 miles	27.0 miles
4. Severe Heat Damage	2.50 miles	7.75 miles	31.0 miles
5. Severe Fire and Wind Damage	3.00 miles	10.0 miles	35.0 miles

4. ***Severe Heat Damage Zone:*** Everything flammable burns in this area. People suffocate since most of the available oxygen is consumed by the fire. Half the people die while another 45% are injured. The overpressure is 6 psi, and the wind velocity comes down to 224 kmph.

5. ***Severe Fire and Wind Damage Zone:*** Here the residential structures are severely damaged. People are blown around and the survivers suffer second and third degree burns. 15% population of this area die and other 50% suffer the burns. The overpressure is 3 psi and the wind velocity is 157 kmph.

Post Nuclear-War Scenario: Ashok kumar writes in ***Hindustan Times*** (May 24, 2002): In a nuclear war there are no victors, only the dead, while survivers will die a slow and torturous death. The only precedent of atomic devastation known to mankind is the dropping of atom bombs over Hiroshima and Nagasaki of Japan. Today's nuclear bombs are on an average 30 times deadlier than those first generation bombs. Today's cities are not sparsely populated towns with mostly single storied structures, but thickly populated with multistoried skyscrapers. This makes the post nuclear-war scenario horribly frightening. If a single nuclear device were to be exploded over a modern city, the blast would rip through skyscrapers turning vast panels and chunks of concrete and steel into high velocity secondary missiles that would smash their way for hundreds of yards in all directions. A nuclear explosion over a city today would affect several thousand areas directly, reducing it instantly to a *smoking crater*. The debris fire ball would be propelled several miles right up to the stratosphere. This could blot out the Sun for several days over vast stretches of land in the subcontinent and the average day temperature would fall by several degrees. This is called the ***Nuclear Winter***. Studies by nuclear scientists show that an extended average drop in temperature by 3 to 4 degree Celsius could destroy the crops over thousands of square miles of land.

The radioactive fallout would result in several million *slow and agonizing deaths*. The only precedents of disaster due to radioactive leak are the *Chernobyl* nuclear plant accident in USSR (now Russia) and Fukushima in Japan. It was a a thousandth fraction of radioactive fallout over Hiroshima. The radioactive cloud over Chernobyl drifted all the way to Europe and reached right up to the coast of the US. There can be no civil defense against the radioactive fallout from a modern nuclear device. The Chernobyl accident overstretched the entire civil defense and emergency resources of the USSR. The cleanup process cost billions of Roubels. One can only shedder to imagine the radioactive fallout from several thousand Chernobyl exploding at the same time. Scientists studying the effects of nuclear radiations confirm that *genetic mutation* is a frightful prospect and the human immune system would be damaged. A detonation over a nuclear power reactor could poison the soil and the underground aquifers, for hundreds or thousands years.

Leading US nuclear scientist *Carl Sagan* says: *Most modern buildings today use large quantities of synthetic material and plastic. A nuclear explosion would set off pyrotoxins, particularly the gamma rays. This is an invisible pyrotoxin, capable of penetrating one foot thick concrete. It is capable of frying the human flesh instantly. The explosion would simultaneously generate a pall of deadly asbestos fibres from high rise buildings insulated with it. The fine asbestos fibre would drift over large areas, exposing multitudes to the long-term prospect of a deadly form of cancer.*

Categories of Nuclear Weapons: Nuclear weapons come in all sizes and configurations. They can be divided into two categories:

1. ***Tactical Nuclear Weapons (TNW):*** Small weapons of sub kiloton yield, that is, bombs with a power of a few hundred or thousand tons of TNT, when configured with appropriate delivery systems (including land based missies with a range of less than 500 kilometers) to be used in the battlefield are called Tactical Nuclear Weapons (TNW). Such low yield devices can be used in the battlefield and would affect a limited area up to few meters. These are the weapons meant for use in limited military maneuvers, such as destroying specific military, communications, or infrastructure targets. In wartime, such explosives could be used for demolishing 'choke points' to enemy offences such as tunnels, narrow mountain passes and long viaducts. TNW include not only *gravity bombs* and short range missiles, but also artillery shells, land mines, depth charges and torpedoes for anti-submarine warfare. Also in this category are nuclear armed ground-based or ship-born surface-to-air missiles (SAM) and air-to-air missiles. This weapon could be fired even from a cannon, even a soldier can carry such bomb and throw it on the target. Small, two-man portable or truck-portable tactical weapons (suitcase weapons), have been developed.

2. ***Strategic Nuclear Weapons (SNW):*** These are nuclear weapons which are designed to be used on targets as a part of strategic plan, such as nuclear missile bases, military command centers and heavy populated civilian areas such as large towns and cities. SNW generally have significantly larger yields, starting from 100 kilotons up to destructive yields in the low megaton range.

The bombs dropped on Hiroshima and Nagasaki (which were gravity bombs of 15 to 20 kiloton yield), though used strategically, are considered tactical weapons by today's standards. Some weapons such as the B61 nuclear bombs are used in both tactical and strategic roles.

A feature of SNW is the greater range of their delivery apparatus, such as ICBM, IBM, etc. The main objective of strategic weapons is the deterrent role, under the theory of ***Mutually Assured Destruction***.

Delivery Systems: The effectiveness of nuclear weapons depends not so much on yield but on the accuracy of the delivery system used. Nuclear weapon delivery is the technology and systems used to place a nuclear weapon at the position of detonation, on or near its target. Several methods have been developed to carry out this task:

Tactical nuclear weapons being of low yield may be launched in standard ordinance shell casings or may even be carried to the battlefield by hand. The higher yield weapons are carried by large vulnerable airplanes.

Air Bombing: Historically, the first method of delivery which was used for the Gravity Bombs—*Little Boy and Fat Man*—dropped at Hiroshima and Nagasaki, was air-dropping by B-29 bomber planes. Many air-dropping techniques exist, including toss bombing, parachute-retarded delivery, and lay down modes, intending to give the dropping aircraft time to escape the ensuing blast. No nuclear weapon can be a Wooden Bomb, that is, a bomb completely trouble free, maintenance free, and danger free under all conditions. Gravity bombs are designed to be dropped from planes, which require that weapon can withstand vibrations and changes in air-temperature and pressure during the course of flight. Early weapons often had a removable core for safety, installed by the air crew during flight. They had to meet safety conditions, to prevent accidental detonation or dropping. A variety of types also had to have a fuse to initiate detonation. Early gravity nuclear bombs could only be carried by the B-29 Super fortress. The next generation weapons were still so big and heavy that could only be carried by bombers such as B-52 Strato fortress and V bombers. But by the mid-1950s smaller weapons had been developed that could be carried and deployed by fighter bombers.

Ballistic Missiles: Today, nuclear devices have been sufficiently miniaturized to fit inside missiles and even howitzers. The strategic nuclear weapons being high yield weapons can be launched through Ballistic Missiles. Missiles using a ballistic trajectory usually deliver a warhead over the horizon. Some ballistic missiles may have a range of hundreds to thousands of kilometers, while large Intercontinental Ballistic Missiles (ICBM), including Submarine-Launched Ballistic Missiles (SLBM), carry out a suborbital spaceflight. An ICBM is more than 20 times as fast as a bomber and more than 10 times as fast as fighter plane. It also flies at a much higher altitude, and therefore more difficult to defend against. ICBM can also be fired quickly in the event of sunrise attack.

Early ballistic missiles carried a single warhead, often megaton-range yield. Since the 1970s modern ballistic weapons have seen the development of far more accurate targeting techniques, particularly due to improvements in *inertial guidance systems*. This set the stage for ICBM with Multiple Independently Targetable Re-entry Vehicles (MIRVs). This was a modern technological wonder. These are multiple warheads and each of these is independently guided to a different target after release by the carrier missile (also called missile bus) at the start of re-entry from space. These are generally carried by ICBMs.

Cruise Missiles: A cruise missile is a jet engine or rocket-propelled missile that flies at low altitude using an automated guidance system to make them hard to detect or intercept. These missiles are extremely accurate, small low flying robotic aircrafts. Cruise missiles can carry a nuclear warhead. They have a shorter range and smaller payloads than ballistic missiles. So their warheads are smaller and less powerful.

Advance Cruise Missile (ACM) AGM-129 is the current nuclear-armed air launched cruise missile. This is carried on the B-52 Stratofortress. This plane can carry 20 missiles. Thus cruise missiles themselves can be compared with MIRV warheads.

Cruise missiles can also be launched from mobile launchers on the ground, and from naval ships, contributing to a surprise factor of attack.

Other Delivery systems: Other potential delivery methods are artillery shells, mines, Blue Peacock, nuclear depth charges and torpedoes. Atomic 'Bazooka' was designed to be used against large formation of tanks. Smaller warhead such as Nike Hercules was developed in 1950s. Also we use air-to-air rockets, AIR-2 Genie etc.

Nuclear War Arsenal: A country intending to become a nuclear power, must have the capability to build up warheads, test facilities, ballistic missiles, Triad—land, air and sea—based delivery systems—for missiles, long range aircrafts, nuclear submarines, radar warning systems, satellite communication systems, air born surveillance systems and command systems. At the same time a really deterrent nuclear power must have full range of nuclear weapons of all sizes and configurations—right from sub kiloton bomb to 20 or more megaton bombs along with a large variety of delivery systems. The delivery systems include not only bomber planes like B-52, B-1 or B-29, but from small range to long range missiles such as IRBMs, ICBMs and the most sophisticated MIRVs, warships and nuclear powered submarines (SSBNs) which are capable of diving deeper, remaining submerged longer and sailing faster and more silently than conventionally powered submarines. SSBNs are generally not detected till launch.

Apart from this, a country needs a force survivable from enemy's nuclear attacks. That is, a force based on railway tracks or deep in mountain silos or onboard nuclear propelled submarines. It should have air defense equipped with a good ***airborne early warning system*** consisting of command and control system and satellite surveillance and targeting system contamination caused by nuclear, biological and chemical weapons but also function as a nuclear shelter. Such systems function effectively in a contaminated area and remove the deadly effects of nuclear bomb attack, just as, radiations coupled with release of extreme heat and rise in air pressure.

Air Born Surveillance System—AWACS

Proliferation of Nuclear Weapons: Nuclear proliferation is a term now used to describe the spread of nuclear weapons, fissile material and weapon-applicable nuclear technology and information, to the nations which are not recognized as 'Nuclear Weapon States' by the nuclear Non-Proliferation Treaty (NPT). In fact, holding on to nuclear arms is not a deterrent but a 'proliferant' that goads others to join the club. Arms control has become a way of avoiding a fate for choice—a world of uncontrolled proliferation or a world with no nuclear weapons at all.

After the initial spell of nuclear explosions at North New Mexico, Hiroshima and Nagasaki in 1945, many felt that knowledge and technique of nuclear bomb manufacturing would remain a closely guarded secret with those initially concerned. But this was not to be. The Second World War was just over. The jingoism amongst the winner countries encouraged them to maintain their power supremacy and humiliating feeling amongst the losers compelled them to come out of depression and somehow restore their early glory. Thus the political jealousy and ambition to become world super-power and also the military and security considerations compelled the various countries to enter the arena of bomb manufacturing. The United States tried its best to monopolize the technology. In 1950, the US Atomic Energy Commission burnt 3000 copies of April issue of *Scientific American* which had already come off the press with the original unmutilated article in its pages by a nuclear physicist Hans Bethe on Hydrogen Bomb. But much of the data had already been published elsewhere and was easily accessible and much of it by Bethe himself. Thus many countries started the work to make their own bomb.

The first major breakthrough came from the Soviet Union (now Russia) which made Atomic and then Hydrogen Bomb. The atomic bomb (RDS-1) was tested on August 29, 1949 in Semipalatinsk (Usturyat desert) and the hydrogen bomb (RDS-6s) on August 12, 1953 in Siberia. Britain, though closely allied to the US decided to have its own nuclear armory. Britain tested its atomic bomb on October 3, 1952 in Bhontebelo island, Australia, and the hydrogen bomb on May 15, 1957 in Chrismus island, Kiribati. Charles de Gaulle strongly felt that France must have its own '*force de frappe*'. He did not want France to be overrun again by the mighty conventional Soviet forces, which were now equipped with nuclear warheads. He felt the need of nuclear deterrent to be used in odd hours. Hence it tested on February 13, 1960 its atomic bomb in Regan, Algeria (which was then under the protection of France) and the hydrogen bomb on August 24, 1968 in Mururao, Fungataad Etol. China was the last to enter the nuclear club in this first round of race. It tested its atomic bomb on October 16, 1964 at Lopnore (Western China) and hydrogen bomb on December 27, 1968 at the same place. Immediately after, these five nuclear powers declared themselves a nuclear club and put 'No Entry' notice on the gate.

China had clear political intentions of becoming one of the world's major powers and went ahead systematically to build up nuclear weapons and missile capabilities. Today it has thermonuclear weapons, ICBMs and Submarine Launched Ballistic Missiles (SLBMs). Following Table 3.2 depicts the status of world nuclear forces and the story of nuclear weapon proliferation. It should be noted that with the exception of Russia and US (which have subjected their nuclear forces to independent verification under various treaties) these figures are estimates, in some cases quite unreliable estimates. The data is from the *Bulletin of the Atomic*

Scientists. In fact the exact number of nuclear weapons in each country's possession is a closely held national secret.

Table 3.2. Status of World Nuclear Forces (2010)

Country	*Strategic*	*Non-Strategic*	*Total Operational*	*Total Inventory*
Five Nuclear-Weapon States under NPT				
Russia	2600	2050	4650	12000
United States	1968	500	2468	9600
France	300	n.a.	~300	300
China	180	?	~180	240
United Kingdom	160	n.a.	<160	185
Non-NPT Nuclear Powers				
Pakistan	70-90	n.a.	n.a.	70-90
India	60-80	n.a.	n.a.	60-80
North Korea	<10	n.a.	n.a.	<10
Undeclared Nuclear Powers				
Israel	80	n.a	n.a.	80
Total	~5400	~2550	~7700	~22600

China found itself to be the king nuclear power in the east and south of the world and started helping countries like Pakistan and Iran in the development of nuclear weapons and missiles against the spirit of Non-Proliferation Treaty NPT) which it had signed.

India, the biggest and strongest country in South Asia and a predominant Power in the entire Indian Ocean rim, but a strong supporter of nuclear disarmament found itself surrounded by China, Pakistan, Iran etc., all indulging in nuclear weaponry activities. At the same time India had already established its nuclear weapon capability by doing a peaceful nuclear experiment (pne) on May 18, 1974. Compelled by security concerns, India, ultimately, came out of self-restrain and tested three nuclear bombs on May 11,

1998 and two more on May 13, 1998. May 11 tests included a 45 kiloton hydrogen bomb. The site for all the tests was Khitoly, a village 35 km from the Pokhran firing range in Rajasthan. Two weeks later on May 28 and May 30 Pakistan also tested half a dozen nuclear devices, in Changai hills of Baluchistan. According to *Sunday Times*, London, CIA (Central Intelligence Agency) has predicted that by the year 2003, Pakistan is likely to have 50 to 75 war heads, while India will have between 75 and 100. Thus India and Pakistan became respectively, the sixth and seventh nuclear club eligible members, but thumping the door with a notice 'No Entry'.

There are other countries believed to have nuclear weapons. Amongst them is Israel. Israel is not a party to NPT and refuses to officially confirm or deny having a nuclear arsenal or having developed nuclear weapons or even having a nuclear weapon program. According to National Resources Defense Council and Federation of American Scientists, Israel likely possesses around 75-100 nuclear weapons.

South Africa produced six nuclear weapons in 1980 but disassembled them in early 1990s.

North Korea, a signatory of NPT, announced a withdrawal from NPT on January 10, 2003, and reported a nuclear test (of less than a kiloton yield) on October 9, 2006. But the general opinion is that the test was probably only partially successful. But on May 25, 2009 North Korea conducted a second, higher yield test.

The United States, under the NATO ***nuclear weapon sharing***, has provided nuclear weapons for Belgium, Germany, Italy, Netherland, Turkey, Canada and Greece, to deploy and store.

There are countries like Belarus, Kazakhstan, Ukrane etc., which were a part of USSR and having about 81, 1400 and 5000 nuclear weapons respectively, returned all of them to Russia after the collapse of Soviet Union in 1991 and subsequently signed the NPT.

19 years after the fall of Soviet Union and the end of the Cold War, the world's combined stockpile of nuclear weapons remains at very high level, approximately 22,330, 95% of these weapons are possessed by the US and Russia alone. 7900 nuclear warheads are now considered deployed and ready for immediate use. 7275 of these warheads reside in the nuclear arsenals of the US and Russia.

A total of approximate 2000 American and Russian strategic nuclear warheads are kept on high alert, quick-launch status. They are mounted on large-range land and sea based ballistic missiles, and kept ready to launch with only a few minutes warning. They can reach their targets anywhere on earth in 30 minutes or less.

A nuclear watchdog organization, *Loss Alamos Study Group* has obtained some leaked Pentagon documents. These documents reveal that the Bush (then US president) administration is planning to overhaul its nuclear arsenal so that it could be used to strike the rogue states' stockpile of chemical and biological arms. According to Greg Mellow of this study group, America is also preparing the ground for a breakaway from global arms control treaties and moratorium on conducting nuclear tests.

The menu of weapons being actively considered is a new generation of nuclear weapons—***mini-nukes, bunker-busters and neutron bombs (ERW, enhanced radiation weapon)***. Mini-nukes, the low yield weapons (tactical warheads of less than a kiloton yield) represent a far more effective deterrent than the existing weapons, as they are more usable. Bunker-busters are earth penetrating weapons, which would break through the earth's surface before detonating. They could be used to destroy chemical or biological arms stored underground. The low yield neutron bombs, as already mentioned in chapter 1, emit stream of neutrons which destroy the tissues or organisms and hence could be used to destroy chemical and biological weapons in surface warehouses.

Mutual Assured Destruction (MAD): Nuclear weapons can compress the fury of war into a few hours and can do monstrous violence. MAD is a Doctrine of military strategy and national security in which a full scale use of nuclear weapons by two opposing sides would effectively result in the destruction of both the attacker and the defender, becoming thus a war that has no victory but only total mutual destruction. It is based upon the theory of deterrence, according to which the deployment of strong weapons is essential to threaten the enemy in order to prevent the use of the same weapons.

The MAD doctrine assumes that each side has enough nuclear weaponry to destroy the other side and that, either side, if attacked for any reason by the other, would retaliate with equal or greater force. The expected result is an immediate escalation resulting in both combatants' total and assured destruction. The doctrine further assumes that neither side will dare to launch a first strike because the other side will launch on warning, with secondary forces (second strike) resulting in the destruction of both parties. The pay off of this doctrine is expected to be a tense but stable peace. Because of its horrendous implications, it serves successfully the purpose of deterrence. It is a symbol of power and not a weapon of war. Its possession is necessary evil.

The war experts are of the view that nuclear weapons are the most effective and cheapest deterrents. In their opinion, the real validity of nuclear weapons lie in their non-use. This simply means that in this nuclearised geo-political environment, nuclear weapons assure a great deal of security, especially when one has the ***second strike*** capability, that is the capability to weather a nuclear first strike and launch an equally devastating nuclear counter strike on the attacker. It follows logically that if the adversaries knew of each other's second strike capability then a first strike would become extremely illogical. Thus MAD, in fact, proved to be a WISE doctrine.

The primary application of MAD is the unremitting hostility (the Cold War) between two super powers without a nuclear war for four decades (1940s to 1990s). A first strike by the U.S. and Russia can destroy about 60 to 70 percent of either of the two countries. Since a first sneak strike can obliterate all land based nuclear missile silos, it is important to deter the first strike by retaining an ability to launch an equally devastating counter strike. This was ensured by either country by keeping nuclear bombers at fail-safe points and by the deployment of the Submarine Launched Ballistic Missiles (SLBMs). Most of these missiles are now housed in nuclear powered submarines (SSBNs) which are, as mentioned earlier, capable of diving deeper, remaining submerged longer and sailing faster and more silently than conventional submarines, hence undetectable till launch.

Cost of Nuclear-Weaponisation: Nuclear programs of every country are shrouded in extreme security. So it is difficult to assess exactly how much a country spends on building and maintaining its nuclear arsenal. Expert's opinion is that the cost of building the bomb itself is not very high, less than Rs. 1 crore. On September 18, 1951, Sen. Brien McMohan, Chairman of the Joint Committee on Atomic energy (JCAE) claimed, "The cost of military fire power based upon atomic bomb is hundreds of time cheaper, dollar for dollar, than conventional explosives". The main costs are in delivering the bomb and in commanding, controlling and defending against the bomb. Also there is lot of expenditure on environmental and waste management.

An assessment of the cost of nuclear defence spendings, by America, over the period of 1940-96 can now be had from a report 'The Cost and Consequences of US Nuclear Weapons since 1940', completed by Brookings Institute of America in August, 1998. According to this report US spends currently 35 billion dollars a year, that is more than 96 million dollars per day. Out of this about 25 billion dollars are spent on operating and maintaining the nuclear arsenal and the remaining are used for managing and cleaning up nuclear waste, verifying arms control agreements and conducting research into ballistic missile defences. The cumulative cost of the US nuclear weapon program is $5.5 trillion. If the US wants to dismantle all these weapons, it has to spend about $300 billion more for management and disposal of nuclear waste. This makes the total $5.8 trillion. The breakdown of total of actual and estimated US expenditure for nuclear weapons (1940-96), as per the report, is given in the following Table 3.3.

Table 3.3. Breakdown of US Expenditure for Nuclear Weapons (1940-96).

Activity	*Cost (billion dollars)*
Building the Bomb	409.4
Deploying the Bomb	3241.0
Targeting and Controlling the Bomb	831.1
Defending against the Bomb	937.2
Dismantling the Bomb	11.1
Nuclear Waste Management and	
Environmental remediation	45.2
Victims of Bomb	2.1
Cost and Consequences of Nuclear energy	3.1
Congressional Oversight of the Bomb	0.9
Total (5.4811 trillion)	5481.1

To give the idea of enormity of this huge amount to a layman, we take this amount in one dollar currency notes, it would stretch over more than 7,27,000 kilometers, all the way to the moon and nearly back again. Moreover, this expenditure exceeds the total federal spending on agriculture, natural resources and environment, education, training, employment and social services, general science and space research, community and regional development, law enforcement and energy production and regulation.

But the actual expenditure on developing and manufacturing nuclear explosives which are more than 70,000 nuclear warheads is only 7 per cent while 86 per cent is the expenditure on deploying offensive and defensive weapons and building the maintaining command, control, communications and intelligence-systems.

Looking at this detailed cost data, only few countries can dare decide to go nuclear. If a country follows the American or Soviet route, its economy will be surely destroyed. If security concerns compel a country to develop its own nuclear weapon, it has to adopt very cautious approach.

❑

4

India Makes the Nuclear Bomb

> ***"India wants peace in the world and it also believes that science is for protection and not for destruction; it should be utilised for development and not for creating trouble. I want to assure that we will proceed in the constructive direction of science."***
>
> ***—Prime Minister Atal Behari Vajpayee.***

History: As early as 26 June, 1946, Pandit Jawaharlal Nehru, soon to be India's first Prime Minister, announced: "As long as the world is constituted as it is, every country will have to devise and use the latest devices for its protection. I have no doubt India will develop her scientific researches and I hope Indian scientists will use the atomic force for constructive purposes. But if India is threatened, she will inevitably try to defend herself by all means at her disposal." Realizing this strategic nature of nuclear power the government set up the Atomic Energy Commission (AEC) in 1948 to produce all the basic material. Dr. Homi Jehangir Bhabha became its first Chairman. The commission first emphasized on peaceful uses of nuclear power and built ***Asia's first atomic research reactor Apsara***, in mid 1950 and set in motion a broad-based nuclear program, and started making radio isotopes on small and research level. When India's second nuclear reactor Cirus (supplied by Canada) started in 1960, Nehru declared, "*We are approaching a stage when it is possible for us .... to make atomic weapons*".

In 1964 India developed the facility to reprocess the spent fuel from Cirus at Trombay. Thus it became world's fifth country able to produce Plutonium. This was sufficient to claim the capability to make nuclear bomb. At this India started working on obtaining electricity from its nuclear reactors. A nuclear power plant started working at Kota, Rajasthan in 1972.

Two years after Chinese aggression on India and four months after the death of Nehru, China conducted its first nuclear test in 1964. On UN day in October, 1964, Dr. Bhabha in a talk broadcast over All India Radio declared authoritatively that India, if decided, could build a nuclear bomb within 18 months. He emphasized that nuclear arms do not constitute an expensive proposition, the delivery systems are not so difficult to acquire. Dr. Bhabha advocated for creating a climate favorable to the countries which have the capability of making atomic bomb but have voluntarily refrained from doing so. Unfortunately, since he spoke, developments have gone in a direction in which India's security needs have increasingly called for nuclear deterrence. Actually, 1962 Sino-Indian war was an eye opener to the Indian establishment. It understood the need to have a strong military with a comprehensive capability to deter enemy forces.

The Chinese Nuclear test at Lopnur in 1964 goaded the Indian government into action to kickstart India's indigenous program to develop nuclear weapons. But the program was shelved after Prime Minister Jawahar Lal Nehru's death only few months back. Meanwhile keeping in mind the 1962 Chinese aggression and 1965 Pakistan aggression on India Lal Bahadur Shastri realized the clouds of insecurity. He tried to seek the nuclear umbrella from England and other nuclear powers but failed. So in 1965 India initiated its own nuclear explosive program. But the sudden death of Shastri and also the death of Dr. Bhabha in a mysterious plane crash in Europe put a break on the nuclear weapon program. Later, the program was reviewed in 1968 by Prime Minister Indira Gandhi. Ultimately, on Buddha Purnima, 1974 India stunned the world and particularly the US by conducting its first underground nuclear test at Pokhran, with the code name *Operation Smiling Buddha*. Due to political pressure India could use an expression for this explosion only a 'Peaceful Nuclear Explosion' (pne). AEC Chairman Dr. Homi Sethna, and director of Bhabha Atomic Research Centre (BARC) Dr. Raja Ramanna were the leading scientists supervising the project.

H.N. Sethna: (August 24, 1923 to September 5, 2010) Homi Nusserwanji Sethna, a nuclear scientist and a chemical engineer, did his schooling from St. Xevier High School, Fort, Mumbai and the University of Michigan Ann Arbor. He was the primary and central figure in India's civilian nuclear program as well as the construction of nuclear power plants. He completed the construction of the Thorium plant and the plant for the production of nuclear grade Uranium metal at Trombay. His first major challenging assignment was the setting up of the Plutonium plant at Trombay in 1959. This was designed and constructed entirely by Indian scientists and engineers under H. N. Sethna as the project engineer. The Uranium Mill at Jaduguda, Bihar was also constructed under his guidance in 1967. He was also the project manager of a 40 MW reactor called Canada-India Reactor in 1956-58.

H.N. Sethna had the full technical responsibility for setting up of the Thorium extraction plant at Alwaye, Kerela, for separation of rare earth from Manazite sands. Sethna was the guiding force behind the first peaceful nuclear explosion, Project Smiling Buddha on May 18, 1974, when he was head of Atomic Energy Commission of India.

H.N. Sethna was honoured with three Indian civilian awards—Padma Shri in 1959, Padma Bhushan in 1966 and Padma Vibhushan in 1975.

Dr. Raja Ramanna: (January 28, 1925—September 21, 2004) born in Tumkur, Karnataka to the parents Rukminiamma and B. Ramanna, was a nuclear scientist and nuclear physicist. His Father was in the judicial service of the Mysore state and earned the reputation of being a kind-hearted judge. Ramanna was associated with the country's first nuclear test in 1974 and research for over 40 years. He is often considered the '*Father of the Indian Nuclear Program*'. Dr. Ramanna was a highly respected scientist in India and Pakistan. A writer Braj Kishore Singh writes: "Raja Ramanna was a talented personality—an eminent nuclear physicist, a highly accomplished technologist, an able administrator, an inspiring leader, a gifted musician, a scholar of Sanskrit literature and philosophy, and above all a complete human being".

Beginning his studies at Bishop Cotton Boy's School, Bangalore, he later graduated from Madrass Christian College and was a resident of St. Thomas's Hall. Raja Ramanna obtained Ph.D. in Nuclear Physics and did a L.R.S.M. from King's College, London. He specialised in nuclear physics, nuclear reactor physics and design, European music and philosophy. Dr. Ramanna was also an accomplished pianist having performed at many public concerts in India and abroad but had a keen ear for Indian classical music.

Dr. Ramanna was the Director of BARC for over a decade. It was during this time that India carried out its first nuclear test in Pokhran in 1974 code named ***Operation Smiling Buddha***. He had served as Director General of the DRDO and as Scientific Adviser to the Defence Minister of India. He was the president of 30th General Conference of the International Atomic Energy Agency (IAEA).

Dr. Ramanna became Union Minister of State for defence in 1990. In 1997, he entered Rajya Sabha. He was also the first Director of National Institute of Advanced studies, Banglore. Government of India awarded him the civilian awards—Padma Shri in 1968, Padma Bhushan in 1973 and Padma Vibhushan in 1975.

A Period of Political Indecision: After Pokhran 1974, the governments in power kept supporting work in this area, but never in an open fashion to inspire confidence either of the armed forces or the public at large. One gave the impression of being afraid of the consequences of firmly going in for the nuclear option. Many sanctions and controls had been imposed in the past, even in areas not related to the nuclear and missile programs. Such consequences are bound to be there and have to be faced.

An accurate picture of the government's attitude towards the scientific community comes from Dr Raja Ramanna. He recalls that Indira Gandhi's ministry refused outright to confer the nation's supreme civilian honour, 'Bharat Ratna' upon Dr. Homi Bhabha. The insulting rebuff was that the Father of India's atomic energy program was not 'big enough'.

But Scientist Continued their Efforts: During a long period of political indecision, the nuclear scientists did not remain idle. They improved upon 1974 version of the bomb and were soon ready with a boosted fission device. In this device the high temperature produced by regular atom bomb is utilized to fuse heavier atoms of Hydrogen and boost the yields tenfold. In 1982-83 Indira Gandhi okayed more nuclear tests. Three shafts were dug for the tests, but at the last minute the tests were called off fearing economic sanctions from western countries. The scientists continued their research. The real problem before them was how to build the bomb to a size that fitted into an aircraft bomb pod and how to regularise and how to ruggedise the device to take the stress of carting and incorporate mechanism to ensure that they do not go off accidentally. The 1974 device was so heavy that only a transport aircraft could deliver it. To achieve the refinement, India's two giant scientific establishments—Defense Research and Development Organisation (DRDO) and Department of Atomic energy (DAE) came together and began to synergize their efforts. As a result, by 1989, India had achieved the ability to drop nuclear bomb using combat aircraft. By 1995 the DRDO and DAE team had made major bomb design changes, reduced its weight and increased its yield. Missiles were developed as safe delivery vehicles. The great scientist A.P.J. Abdul Kalam had all praises for the great partnership and described it through a simple equation:

Nuclear technology + defense technology
= nuclear weapon technology and systems

In December, 1995 again the tests were planed but were halted after American satellites picked up signs of preparations for testing at Pokhran. The Americans under President Bill Clinton exerted enormous pressure on Narsinmha Rao (the then Prime Minister of India) to stop the preparations and Rao bucked out under the pressure.

While the threat of sanctions was being cleverly employed to rein in India, the country had over the years, fallen victim to increasing technology sanctions for merely retaining an open nuclear option. Energy cost benefit analysis was indicating that India was bleeding its interests, increasing the liabilities of maintaining the open option but not making the security gains.

The ***turning point*** came when openly pro-nuclear government took office in March, 1998 with Atal Behari Vajpayee as the Prime Minister. This government knew that continued inaction would bring India under stepped up pressure from next year with the Comprehensive Test Ban Treaty (CTBT) coming into force from September, 1999 and the Non Proliferation Treaty (NPT) review conference in 2000. The government also realized that any testing plan would get leaked to the US unless it was confined to a handful of decision makers.

Preparations for the Tests

Therefore, the scientists involved in the operation took care to ensure that even their closed friends and colleagues would not detect the work being undertaken at Pokhran. All of them did not depart for Pokhran simultaneously, but left in groups of two or three. One group would use the pretext of attending a seminar or conference, and would tell their wives that they could not be contacted while they were away. Tickets were bought for a destination other than Pokhran (or cities nearby) under pseudonyms, and after arriving at their destination, the group would secretly leave for the military basin, Jaisalmer from where they would be taken by the army to Pokhran. After the return of one group, another group would leave for the range employing similar means to do their work. All technical staff at the test range, wore military fatigues, so that in spy satellite images they would appear to be military personnel maintaining the test range as usual.

On the diplomatic front, the foreign secretary K. Raghunath and Defence Minister George Fernandes, in their separate meetings with American officials stated that India has not yet decided about going nuclear. They also conveyed to the officials that the National Security Council would be meeting on 26th May to discuss the matter and decide about the nuclear option. All this led the Americans and the world community not to take BJP's compaign promises seriously and hence did not expect an Indian nuclear test so soon.

Production and Preparation of Devices

Three laboratories of the DRDO—testing and producing components like advanced detonators, the implosion Systems, high-voltage trigger systems—were involved in designing. They were also responsible for weaponisation, system engineering, aerodynamics, safety interlocks and flight trials.

Nuclear devices were taken out from BARC on May 1, at around 3 a.m. by four army trucks under the command of Col.

Umang Kapoor. They were transported to Mumbai airport and flown at dawn in an Indian Air force AN-32 transport plane to the Jaisalmer military base. An army convoy of 4 trucks transported the explosive devices to Pokhran. The devices were delivered directly to the device preparation building in the range, designated as ***Prayer Hall***.

The first group of three devices was tested on May 11 and the second group of two devices was tested on May 13. All the five devices were placed in different shafts. Shakti-I, a thermonuclear device was placed in a 200 meter deep shaft code named ***White House***; *Shakti-II*, a fusion bomb was placed in another (over 150 meter deep) shaft named ***Taj Mahal*** and the third shaft named ***Kumbhkaran*** was assigned to *Shakti-III*, the first sub-kiloton bomb *Shakti-IV and Shakti-V* of the second group of tests were placed in shafts code named ***NT-I and NT-II*** respectively.

It was again a Buddha Purnima May 11, 1998 at 3:45 PM, when India conducted three under ground nuclear tests within minutes of each other at Pokhran. This stunned the world and exposed one of America's biggest intelligence failures. Subsequently, on May 13 at 12:21 PM, India tested two more highly sophisticated devices with sub-kiloton yields. These two blasts showed that India can do advanced thermonuclear tests which are limited to sub-critical or slightly supercritical neutron multiplication and release negligible amount of fission energy.

Dust Columns from the Shakti Test Series May 11, 1998

Announcement by the Prime Minister: On Monday, May 11, 1998, Prime Minister Shri Atal Bihari Vajpayee declared, "I have an announcement to make, today at 3:45 PM, India conducted three underground nuclear tests in the Pokhran range (in Rajasthan state). These were contained explosions like the experiment conducted in May, 1974."

He went on to say that the devices tested were a thermonuclear device, a fusion device, and a low-yield device.

"I warmly congratulate the scientists and engineers who have carried out these successful tests."

Later, he declared, "*That India is a nuclear weapon state is a reality which cannot be denied. It is not a conferment that we seek; nor is it a status for others to grant. It is an endowment to the nation by our scientists and engineers*."

Main Personnel Involved in the Operation:

Project Chief Coordinators:

- Dr. A.P.J. Abdul Kalam: Scientific Adviser to the Prime Minister and head of the Defence Research and Development Organization.
- Dr R. Chidambaram: Chairman of the Atomic Energy Commission and Department of Atomic Energy.

Bhabhha Atomic Research Center:

Dr. Anil Kakodkar, Director of Bhabha Atomic Research Centre.

- Dr. Satinder Kumar Sikka, Director, Thermonuclear Weapon Development.
- Dr. M.S. Ramkumar, Director of Nuclear Fuel and Automation Manufacturing Group; Director, Nuclear-Component Manufacture.
- Dr. D. D. Sood, Director of Radio Chemistry and Isotopic Group. Director, Nuclear Materials Acquisition.
- Dr. S.K. Gupta, Solid State Physics and Spectroscopy group, Director, Device Design and Assessment.
- Dr. G. Govindraj, Associate Professor of Electronic and Instrumentation Group, Director, Field Instrumentation.

Defence Research and Development Organization

- Dr. K. Santhanam, Director, Test Site Preparations.
- Dr. M. Vasudev, Range Safety Officer.
- Regiment 58 Engineers.

Secret of Secrecy of Operation Shakti: Where America was furious against India on Pokhran-II explosions, it was also angry with his own spying system. American intelligence department equipped with worldwide spying network and snooping spy satellites could not smell even a trace of preparations for Indian nuclear tests. Some of the steps taken by India to keep its mission a secret have been given earlier and other few are listed below.

- India deliberately chose the month of May for these tests, because there are dust storms prevailing for days together in the Pokhran desert. The spy satellites cannot watch any activity on the ground, the dust blind their eyes. The tier prints due to vehicular movements are immediately covered by the dust, otherwise only photographs of these tier prints are sufficient to indicate some secret activity.

Camouflaged well for testing the bomb

- In this month, the day temperature in these areas reaches 50°C. At this temperature the heat waves (which are nothing but Infra Red rays) emitted by hot ground surface create a sort of invisible 'fog' in the atmosphere through which satellite spy cameras (infrared cameras) cannot see. The photographs taken by these cameras are blurred. So they become totally redundant.
- Due to the information provided by India's IRS (Indian Remote Sensing) series state satellites, the 'where and when' information about the American spy satellites was known. Therefore when the American satellites would pass over Pokhran, the devices installed in the fields were camouflaged.

India played another trick. Along with Shakti operation, our scientists simultaneously started a rigorous activity at missile testing station at Chandipur, situated in the distant east from Pokhran. India actually test-fired short range triple-role 'Trishul' missile at around 1:00 AM at the interim test-range (ITR) at Chandipur on May 11, 1998. In this way, the spy satellites fixed their cameras on Chandipur and Pokhran remained away from their sight.

Scientists and Soldiers at Pokhran?

- It is well known that Indian army's one of the firing ranges is situated in Pokhran. So the soldiers have been coming and going frequently from this place. Therefore, throughout the operation period all civilians had been visiting that place with assumed names and donned military uniforms. A.P.J. Abdul Kalam and R. Chidambaram used to visit that place in the disguise of Major General Prithviraj and Major General Natraj respectively. So nobody could realize that this soldier's activity was actually a scientific activity.
- It is learnt that the leader of operation SHAKTI, A.P.J. Abdul Kalam has keen interest in the world of planets. He found that the planetary positions during this period were the same as those were during 1974 test.

Shakti Declarations: In a joint statement on May 17, 1998, Dr. Kalam and R. Chidambaram issued the details of the five explosions:

The five devices were placed in separate holes. The thermonuclear (45 kiloton), fission (15 kiloton) and low yield (0.2 kiloton) devices on May 11, were detonated simultaneously, and two more sub-kiloton devices (0.5 and 0.3 kiloton) were simultaneously triggered on May 13.

Kalam and Chidambaram at Press Conference

The thermonuclear device and the fission devices had been placed in shafts distanced only by a kilometer. It was, therefore, necessary to go in for simultaneous detonation in order to save the other shafts from being damaged.

The Hydrogen Bomb was a two stage device having a fission trigger and a secondary fusion device. This was not a boosted fission device as the West had been speculating. The later device does not have a secondary stage. They also claimed that the Thermo-nuclear device gave a total yield of 45 kiloton, 15 kiloton from the fission trigger and 30 kiloton from the fusion process and that the theoretical yield of the device (200 kiloton) was reduced to 45 kiloton in order to minimize seismic damage to villages near the test range. The village nearest to the test range, Khetolai, was a mere 5 kilometer away.

It was a low-cost affair and the cost was shared by DRDO and DAE, out of their budgetary resources. 'Remote detonation' of three nuclear devices from a distance of 7 kilometers has never been done by anyone before.

India's nuclear weaponisation was complete and only the command and control systems—already existing in different forms—required consolidation.

'Remote detonation' of three nuclear devices from a distance of 7 kilometers has never been done by anyone before.

India's nuclear weaponisation was complete and only the command and control systems—already existing in different forms—required consolidation.

These tests have provided the critical data for the validation of India's capability to design nuclear weapons of different yields for different applications and different delivery systems.

These tests have significantly enhanced our capability to computer simulations of new designs and taken us to the stage of sub-critical experiments in the future, if considered necessary.

They also clarified that the fissile material was fabricated to suitable shapes by BARC and the high energy explosives used in all the tested devices for attaining critical mass had come from the DRDO, and hence declared, "*India has qualified as nuclear weapon state under clause 9 of the NPT*".

The description **of Shakti** test devices is given briefly in the Table 4.1.

Table 4.1. Shakti Test Devices

Identifier	*Description*
Shakti 1	Two stage thermonuclear device with fusion boosted primary, intended for missile warhead, test design yield 45 kiloton with a 200kt deployed yield.
Shakti 2	Light weight pure fission tactical bomb/missile war head, 12 kiloton design yield.
Shakti 3	Fission experimental device, reportedly made with reactor-grade Plutonium, probably a fusion boosted design without the fusion fuel, 0.3 kiloton design yield.
Shakti 4	0.5 kiloton experimental device.
Shakti 5	0.2 kiloton experimental device.

Unnecessary Controversy: On the completion of these tests, the West could not absorb India's success easily particularly the success in making the Hydrogen Bomb. So they doubted the actual type and yield of this bomb. They said, this was not a Thermo Nuclear device but a Boosted Fission Bomb and the yield was much less than claimed by Indian Government. These doubts were clarified in the Joint Statement as given above. To repeat, they said that the Hydrogen Bomb was a two-stage device having a fission trigger and a secondary fusion device, which gave a total yield of 45 kiloton, 15 kiloton from the fission trigger and 30 kiloton from the fusion process and that the theoretical yield of the device (200 kiloton) was reduced to 45 kiloton in order to minimize damage to the villages nearby. The village nearest to the test range, Khetolai, was a mere 5 kilometer away. Unfortunately on August, 2009, atomic scientist K. Santhanam who was, as we know, closely associated with the tests gave (after retirement) a statement that 1998 tests were not successful as the BJP Government had claimed. This statement was widely dismissed in India, including a specific dismissal by former Indian President and Nuclear Physicist A.P.J. Abdul Kalam, who cited evidence and data to prove his point.

National Technology Day: May 11 has been officially declared as *National Technology Day* in India to commemorate the first of the five tests that were carried out on May 11, 1998. The day was officially signed by the then Prime Minister of India. The day is celebrated by giving awards to various individuals and industries in the field of Science and Industry.

Foundations of Nuclear Establishment: India's nuclear power and weapon generation program is based on very good foundations. It has gone on steadily to develop its capabilities on a self-reliant basis in the field of nuclear science and technology. This covers the entire nuclear range—exploration, mining, extraction, purification and conversion of nuclear materials; production of fuel elements; design and construction of power reactors; production of heavy water; health and safety; instrumentation; isotope separation and all related capabilities in physics, chemistry, biology, engineering, and electronics. The technological know-how and capabilities and various facilities established across this spectrum enabled to do all what is known as Pokhran I, II and III.

There should be no doubt that the success achieved in the fields of nuclear energy, space and defence research and development is essentially the outcome of certain elements so clearly outlined by our great scientist Homi Jehangir Bhabha. He was a great administrator as well as a scientist. He had a great vision and very clear understanding of the difference between the administration required for the growth of science and technology than that required for the operation of industrial enterprises. Not only this, he even understood the difference between both of these administrations and the type of administration required for preservation of law and order, justice, finance etc. In January, 1966, he said in his concluding address to the International Council of Scientific Unions meeting in Mumbai, "It is my personal view, which is shared by many eminent foreign scientists, that the general absence of proper administrative set up for science is a bigger obstacle to the rapid growth of science and technology than the paucity of scientists and technologists, because a majority of these experts we have are made less effective through the lack of the right type of administrative support". The atomic energy, space and defence research and development agencies have always been led by scientists. The entire culture of functioning of these departments is different from that of the normal bureaucratic system. Administrators who are dedicated, committed, intelligent and understand the rationale behind the functioning of these agencies, ensure the right type of support. The Council of Scientific and industrial Research (CSIR) is somewhat similar.

Homi Bhabha Biography: Homi Jahangir Bhabha was born in a rich Parsi family on October 30, 1909 in Mumbai. He was graduated from Elphinston College and the Royal Institute of Science in Mumbai. In 1934 he received his Doctorate from Cambridge University. During this period he worked with Niels Bohr on the studies that led to Quantum Theory. Homi J. Bhabha aiso worked with Walter Heitler on the Cascade Theory of electron showers. He did significant work in identifying ***Meson.***

Homi Bhabha

In 1939 Second World War broke out, so Bhabha returned to India and set up the Cosmic Ray Research Unit at the Indian Institute of Science, Bangalore under C.V. Raman. He also established the Tata Institute of Fundamental Research (TIFR) in Mumbai, with the help of J.R.D. Tata. In 1945, he became the director of TIFR.

Homi Jahangir Bhabha was not only a great scientist, as stated earlier, he was a skilled administrator. After independence he, with the blessings of Jawahar Lal Nehru dedicated himself for peaceful development of atomic energy. In 1948 he established the Atomic Energy Commission of India and was made its First Chairman.

Under his guidance, ***Apsara***, the first atomic reactor in Asia, went into operation at Trombay (near Mumbai) in 1956.

Bhabha chaired the first United Nations Conference held in Geneva in 1955. He pleaded for international control of nuclear energy and the outlawing of atomic bombs by all countries. He wanted nuclear energy to be used for removing poverty and misery of people. He was member of National Academy of Science in the United States. Homi Jahangir Bhabha died in an aeroplane crash in Switzerland on January 24, 1966.

Along with foundation maker Dr. Bhabha, there are a number of other scientists who equally dedicated their lives to the Indian nuclear establishments.

Rajagopal Chidambaram: Dr. Chidambaram, an experimental physicist and crystallographer of international repute, is one of those few scientists who were involved in all the six nuclear tests conducted by India. He built a strong high pressure physicists group involved in designing the configuration of the various devices during the Shakti Operations. Later he became adviser to the defence minister. He has been unanimously declared father of *Pokhran*-II by the Indian Nuclear Scientist Community. He was awarded Padma Bhushan in 1975 in recognition of his services toward Pokhran-I, and the second highest civilian award, Padma Vibhushan in 1999 for his brilliant role in Pokhran-II and *Pokhran*-III.

He was born on December 11, 1936 at Chennai. As far as his academic record, he has been a brilliant and intelligent student. In 1956, he received the Honors degree in physics from Madrass

(Chennai) University in first division. Later he maintained this position in Postgraduate Degree also. Indian Institute of Science awarded him the Martin Forster medal for his marvelous thesis. Rajgopal's father, who was an accountant in the ministry of defence, wanted him to do I.A.S., but he was interested in nuclear physics. R. Chidambaram is shy to face media and has a keen interest in Cricket and Tennis. During leisurely hours he listens to Karnataka music.

R. Chidambaram is a researcher of very high class. When America was boasting at his Super Computer, it was he who gifted India a super computer, ***Anupam***.

He started his carrier in 1962 by joining BARC, as a crystallographer. In 1994, he was member adviser to International Atomic Energy Agency (IAEA) and subsequently was promoted to become the chairman of its board of directors. In 1995 he was made Chairman of AEC. He gave an important contribution to the development of Advance Reactor System.

Dr. Chidambaram is highly disciplined and a man dedicated to the Indian nuclear program. During operation Shakti of 1998 his dedication towards successful completion of nuclear tests was so intense that he could not spare time even for his family. He was in Mumbai on April 29 in connection with the marriage of his second daughter. After two days, he went to New Delhi to attend the meeting of the Cabinet and Planning Commission. On May 4, he returned to Mumbai to see his daughter off to Bhopal and on May 11 he reached back to Pokhran. During this period he met a large number of his friends and relatives but nobody could smell the importance of the period he was passing through. He was alert so much about the secrecy of his mission that his own family members were as much astonished at the nuclear explosion as the other common people.

Dr. Avul Pakir Jainulabdeen (A.P.J.) Abdul Kalam: Abdul Kalam was born on 15th October, 1931 at Rameswaram in Tamil Nadu. He graduated in aeronautical engineering from the Madrass Institute of Technology in 1958 and joined the Defence Research and Development Organisation (DRDO). In 1962, Kalam joined Indian Space Research Organisation (ISRO) and rejoined DRDO in 1982 as the chief executive of Integrated Guided Missile Development Program (IGMDP). Dr. Kalam was the project director of India's first indigenous Satellite Launch Vehicle (SLV-III) and hence is known as the ***Missile Man of India***. He is credited with development and operationalisation of India's ***Agni and Prithvi*** missiles.

He worked as the Scientific Advisor to the Defence Minister and secretary, department of Defence Research and Development from 1992 to 1999. He became the driving force behind the project to weaponise the country's nuclear capability and headed the group of scientists who conducted the Pokhran-II and Pokhran-III nuclear tests. From November 1999 to November 2001 Dr. Kalam was Scientific Adviser to the government of India. Dr. Kalam was elected India's 11th President on July 25, 2002.

In November, 2001 Dr. Kalam took up teaching at Anna University, Chennai. He is a prolific author. He wrote—***Wings of Fire, India 2020 – A Vision for the New Millennium, My Journey, and Ignited Minds—Unleashing the Power within India.***

He is a favourite with children all over the country. Dr. Kalam was awarded the Padma Bhushan in 1981, Padma vibhushan in 1990 and the Bharat Ratna in1997. Dr. Kalam became India's first president who undertook the undersea journey in the INS Sindhurakshak submarine and to undertake a sortie in a fighter aircraft, Sukhoi-30 MK1.

Anil Kakodkar: Born on November11, 1943 in Barwani

(presently in Madhya Pradesh) to Gandhian freedom fighter parents, Smt. Kamla and Purushottam Kakodkar, Anil kakodkar is an eminent Indian nuclear scientist and mechanical engineer. After having his earlier education in Barwani, Kakodkar graduated from Ruparel College, Mumbai University with a degree in Mechanical Engineering in 1963. He also obtained a master degree in Experimental Stress Analysis from the university of Nottingham in 1969.

Anil Kakodkar joined the Reactor Engineering Division of the Bhabha Atomic Research Centre (BARC) and played a key role in design and construction of the *Dhruva* reactor, a completely original but high-tech project where much of India's weapon grade Plutonium is extracted. He has led the indigenous development of India's Pressurised Heavy Water Reactor Technology. His work in the rehabilitation of the two reactors at Kalapakkam and the first unit at Rawatbhatta, which at one stage were on the verge of being written off, are examples of his engineering capability. In 1966 he became director of the BARC and since 2000 he has been leading the Atomic Energy Commission (AEC) of India and also was the secretary of the Department of Atomic Energy (DAE). He has published over 250 scientific papers. He like Chidambaram, was a part of the core team of architects of India's Peaceful Nuclear Experiment in 1974 and Pokhran tests of 1998.

Today, Kakodkar continues to engage in designing the Advanced Heavy Water Reactor that uses Thorium-Uranium 233 as primary energy source and Plutonium as the driver fuel. This unique reactor system, with simplified but safe technology, will generate 75% of electricity from Thorium. If Kakodkar's dream comes true, it will solve India's energy crisis.

K. Santhanam: Santhanam is an atomic energy scientist specialising in reactor hazards evolution. For many years he has been tracking China and Pakistan's nuclear programs and helping the External Affairs Ministry in policy making. He joined DRDO in 1986 and enhanced country's electronic warfare and war gaming capabilities. In 1988, he was asked to coordinate the efforts to weaponise India's nuclear capability. He efficiently and effectively coordinated and integrated the technological strengths of DRDO and DAE resulting in the successful nuclear explosions in 1998 at Pokhran.

❑

5

India's Nuclear Prowess

> ***"There is no compromise on national security. We will exercise all options including nuclear options to protect security and sovereignty."***
>
> ***— Prime Minister designate Atal Behari Vajpayee.***

India's Nuclear Arsenal: Though India has not made any official statement about the size of its nuclear arsenal, estimates suggest that India has between 40 and 95 nuclear weapons, consistent with estimates that it has produced enough weapon grade Plutonium for up to 75 to 110 nuclear weapons. Production of weapon grade Plutonium is believed to be taking place at the BARC, which is home to the CIRUS reactor acquired from Canada, to the indigenous DHRUV reactor, and to a Plutonium separation facility. The Commander-in-Chief of the US strategic nuclear forces, General Eugene Habiger feels that India (and Pakistan) will need at least three to five years (by the year 2001 to 2003) to upgrade themselves from being capable of nuclear tests to nuclear weaponisation.

According to an authoritative defence journal '*Jane's Intelligence Review*' India's potential nuclear arsenal is bigger than that of Britain and in the same league as that of the French and Chinese. In its July, 1998 edition, the journal wrote, "Nuclear tests conducted by India last month have provided crucial information suggesting that the country could build hundreds of nuclear weapons.

India's nuclear weapon program was based primarily on weapon grade Plutonium reprocessed from irradiated fuel taken from two research reactors at Trombay".

In an article W.P. Sidhu, a specialist on South Asian security issues, writes, "Based on the fissile material out of these two reactors alone, India's nuclear weapon stockpile can be put at anything between at least 20 weapons to at the most 65 weapons".

Norris Robert S. and Hans M. Kristenson, in *Bulletin of the Atomic Scientists* estimated in 2005 that India had 40 to 50 warheads. The same bulletin gave the estimate, in November, 2008 that India has about 70 assembled nuclear warheads, with about 50 of them fully operational. A report by David Albright, published by the *Institute of Science and International Security* in 2000, estimated that India at the end of 1999 had 310 kg of weapon grade plutonium, enough for 65 nuclear weapons. He also estimated that India had 4200 kg of reactor grade Plutonium which is enough to build 1000 nuclear weapons. By the end of 2004, he estimates India had 445 kg of weapon grade Plutonium which is enough for around 85 nuclear weapons, considering 5 kg of Plutonium required for each weapon.

Former RAW official J.K. Sinha, claimed that India is capable of producing 130 kg of weapon grade Plutonium per year from six *Unsafeguarded* reactors not included in the nuclear deal between India and the United States.

India's Nuclear Reactors: The nuclear prowess of a country is also assessed on the basis of the number of nuclear reactors it has. India has ten nuclear power reactors, most of them are built by its own scientists. [Rawatbhatta (Rajasthan), Kalapakkam (Tamil Nadu), Narora (U.P.)-2 plants, Kakrapar (Gujarat)-2 plants, Tarapur (Maharashtra), Kaiga (Karnataka), Kundankulam (Tamil Nadu)-2 plants]. A Canadian company supplied to India a reactor 'Candu' and halted construction on the second when India conducted pne in 1974. India completed the second Canadian reactor on its own in 1981 and built additional heavy water reactors with different features. According to a Canadian expert the safety shut down system and radiation containment structures of the Indian-built reactors, are vastly different than those of Candu design. According to I.S. Gopi Rethinaraj, a writer for *Jane's Intelligence Review* on nuclear issues, two reactors at Chennai, two at Narora and two at Kakrapar were built indigenously but were all based on the basic Candu design which uses natural Uranium as fuel and heavy water as moderator.

Detailed list of India's 22 commercial nuclear power reactors and 6 research reactors is given in Table 5.1

Table 5.1. India's Nuclear Reactors

Location	*Unit Name*	*Capacity (MW)*	*Type*	*Reactor Supplier*	*Date of Operation*
Kaiga	Kaiga1	220	PHWR	NPCIL	11/2000
	Kaiga 2	220	PHWR	NPCIL	03/2000
	Kaiga 3	220	PHWR	NPCIL	05/2007
(Karnataka)	Kaiga 4	220	PHWR	NPCIL	03/2009*
Kakrapar	Kakra-par1	220	PHWR	DAE/ NPCIL	05/1993
(Gujarat)	Kakra-par 2	220	PHWR	DAE/ NPCIL	09/1995
Kalapakkam	Kalapakkam 1	220	PHWR	DAE	01/1984
(Tamil Nadu)	Kalapakkam 2	220	PHWR	DAE	03/1986
Kota	Rajasthan 1	100	PHWR	AECL	12/1973
	Rajasthan 2	200	PHWR	AECL/ DAE	04/1981
	Rajasthan 3	220	PHWR	NPCIL	06/2000
	Rajasthan 4	220	PHWR	NPCIL	12/2000
	Rajasthan 5	220	PHWR	NPCIL	02/2009*

(Rajasthan)	Rajasthan 6	220	PHWR	NPCIL	06/2009*
Kundankulam	Kundankulam 1	1000	PWR	Russia	08/2009*
(Tamil- Nadu)	Kundankulam 2	1000	PWR	Russia	05/2010*
Narora	Narora 1	220	PHWR	NPCIL	01/1991
(UP)	Narora 2	220	PHWR	NPCIL	07 /1992
Tarapur	Tarapur 1	160	BWR	GE	11/1969
	Tarapur 2	16	BWR	GE	11/1969
	Tarapur 3	540	PHWR	NPCIL	08/2006
(Maharashtra)	Tarapur 4	540	PHWR	NPCIL	09/2005
	Apsara**	1	PWR	UK	08/1956
	Cirus**	40	PHWR	Canada	1960
	Dhruva**	100	PHWR	BARC	11/1969
(Research Reactors)	FBTR	100	Sodium cooled	DAE	07/1997
	Kamini	100	Sodium cooled	DAE	1989
	(Proto-type)	500	Sodium cooled	DAE	2009*

* All the six reactors against which the date of completion is marked with *, are complete upto more than 90% and are expected to be completed fully by 2009-2010.

** Apsara, Cirus, Dhruva and prototype FBR reactors are utilized by BARC. All other commercial and research reactors utilized by the places where they are situated.

** Amongst the research reactors Apsara is slated to be moved out of BARC complex where it is situated at present.

** Dhruva reactor is capable of producing up to 30 kg of weapon grade Plutonium each year. It is likely that most Indian nuclear warheads use Plutonium extracted from this research reactor.

** BARC has announced plans to replace the aging Cirus and Dhruva. A 100 MW reactor based on Dhruva design is expected to become operational by 2010.

Fast Breeder Test Reactor (FBTR) uses indigenously developed mixed Uranium-Plutonium Carbide fuel.

The ***Kamini*** reactor is the only reactor in the world fueled by U^{233} (irradiated core Thorium) and is the part of India's strategy to eventually use U^{233} as the primary fuel for India's nuclear program.

Another preliminary plan has been completed for building a new 500 megawatt electric (MWe) Advanced Heavy Water Reactor (AHWR) that will burn mixed-oxide (MOX) and Thorium fuel.

Indo-US Nuclear Deal: Due to the Indo-US nuclear deal, 2008 India plans to place 14 out of 22 commercial nuclear power reactors under international safeguards. At present two reactors each at Rawatbhatta (in Rajasthan), Kundankulam and Tarapur built with Canadian, Russia and US assistance respectively are already under safeguards. Under this agreement all future commercial power reactors will also be placed under international safeguards. The research reactor Apsara and the one with research facilities at Kalapakkam will not be under safeguards.

Chemical Weapons: In 1992 India signed Chemical Weapon Convention (CWC). By doing this India became one of the original signatories of CWC in 1993 and ratified it on September 2, 1996.

According to India's ex-Army Chief General Sunderji, a country having the capability of making nuclear weapons does not need to have chemical weapons, since the dread of chemical weapons could be created only in those countries that do not have nuclear weapons. Others suggested that the fact that India has found chemical weapons dispensable, highlighted its confidence in the conventional weapons system at its command.

India informed the United Nations in May, 2009 that it had destroyed its stockpile of chemical weapons in compliance with the International Chemical Weapons Convention. With this India has become third country after South Korea and Albania to do so.

Biological Warfare: India has a well developed biotechnology infrastructure that includes numerous pharmaceutical production facilities, bio-containment laboratories (including BSL-3 and BSL-4) for working with lethal pathogens. It has also highly qualified scientists with expertise in infectious diseases. Some of India's facilities are being used to support research and development for Biological War defence purposes.

India has ratified the Biological War Convention (BWC) and pledges to abide by its obligations. Now Delhi does possess the scientific capability and infrastructure to launch an offensive BW program, but has chosen not to do so. In terms of delivery, India also possesses the capability to produce aerosols and has numerous potential delivery systems ranging from crop dusters to sophisticated ballistic missiles. India has no interest in delivery of biological agents by these or any other means. To reiterate the latter point, in October, 2002, Indian President A.P.J. Abdul Kalam asserted that "We (India) will not make Biological Weapons. It is cruel to human beings."

Nuclear Weapons Delivery Systems: India posseesses nuclear weapons and maintains short- and intermediate-range ballistic missiles, nuclear capable aircrafts, surface ships and submarines under development as possible delivery systems and platforms. Although it lacks an operational ballistic missile submarine, India has ambition of possessing a ***Nuclear Triad*** in the near future when INS Arihant the lead ship of India's Arihant class of nuclear powered submarines formally joins the Indian navy in 2012 after undergoing extensive sea-trials.

Indian Missile Program: Apart from lack of political will, a key constraint on India going overtly nuclear was its lack of missile capability. As explained earlier also, the essence of deterrence is its second strike ability. That is its ability to retaliate with devastating might after surviving a first strike by enemy. A nuclear deterrence is centered on missiles, not on bomber-aircrafts which, in case of India, cannot reach even the heartland of its leading security concerned, China. Realising this, the country instituted the ballistic missile developing program in 1983. Actually India's nuclear option opened up in operational sense only in February, 1994 when Agni was flight tested completing its triumphant three-test developmental phase. It should be noted that the first Agni test was carried out in 1989 despite threatening punitive sanctions from certain foreign powers. Dr. Kalam said in 1994 that Agni needs no further experimental flight tests but only 'random batch tests', once its production begins.

With the advance of simulation technology, longer range missiles are entering production after one to four flight tests. The Agni comprises two stages, each tested many times. Its solid fuel first stage is the SLV-3 space launcher, while its liquid fuel second stage is the Prithvi. Agni-type missiles make strategic sense only if they carry a nuclear weapon. A week after Pokhran 1998 explosions India's missile man, Dr. Kalam announced that both Agni and Prithvi missiles were capable of carrying conventional and nuclear warheads. The country had the capability, successfully demonstrated in the recent sub-kiloton nuclear tests, to miniaturize the nuclear warheads so that it could be fitted on any missile.

In a joint press conference of DRDO and DAE, Dr. Kalam also announced that India has made a quantum technological leap in the weapons delivery systems, with several variants of extended range surface-to-surface Agni IRBMs being developed by DRDO. The project has already reached an advanced stage of development. If needed, it can be made in required numbers. It has also been officially announced that DRDO has the capability to built Agni which could be propelled on solid-solid, liquid-liquid and solid-liquid fuel combinations. Effectively it means that India now has a long range missile catagorised as an intermediate range missile. The new version of Agni could take care of the missile threat posed by China.

While India had demonstrated its delivery capability, it had not demonstrated its ability to build a nuclear warhead for the Agni. A reliable warhead could never have emerged without testing. In fact without the testing option, India would have had no nuclear option worth the name.

India has methodically built an indigenous missile production capability, using its commercial space-launch program to develop the skills and infrastructure needed to support an offensive ballistic missile program. For example, during the 1983s, India conducted a series of space launches using the solid-fueled SLV-3 booster. Most of these launches put light satellites into near-earth orbit. Elements of the SLV-3 were subsequently incorporated into two new programs. In the first, the new Polar Space Launch Vehicle (PSLV) was equipped with six SLV-3 motors strapped to the PSLV's first stage. The Agni IRBM technology demonstrator uses the SLV-3 booster at its first stage.

***Integrated Guided Missile Development Program (IGMDP)*:** This Indian Ministry of Defence program has been developing since 1983 under the former President Dr. Abdul Kalam for the development of a comprehensive range of missiles including Akash and Trishul (surface-to-air) Nag (anti-tank missile) the intermediate range Agni and short range missiles such as Prithvi. Other projects such as Indian Ballistic Missile Defence Program (IBMDP) have derived from the IGMDP. In 2005, India became only the fourth country to have anti-ballistic capability when India tested two systems the AAD (Advanced Air Defence) and PAD (Prithvi Air Defence).

Surface-Air Missile:

Akash *(the sky)* is India's surface-to-air medium range missile defence system. The missile can target aircraft upto 30 kilometers away, at altitude up to 1800 meters. Akash can be fired from both tracked and wheeled platforms. Akash is said to be capable of both conventional and nuclear warheads, with a reported payload of 60 kg. A nuclear waerhead could potentially give the missile the capability to destroy both aircraft and warheads from ballistic missiles. The missile is described as being able to strike several targets simultaneously, which could mean either separate, independently targetable warheads, or a sufficient blast to destroy a number of them.

Akash

Trishul is sea-skimming.

Nag *(Cobra)* is anti-tank missile. The first successful test firing of 6 kilometer range Nag with an Imaging Infrared (IIR) homing guidance system with a *fire-and-forget*[1] capability was done in September, 1997. The Nag is fitted with a tandem High Explosive Anti-Tank (HEAT) warhead to penetrate an Explosive

1. A fire-and-forget principle missile, unlike other conventional guided missiles, has a smart computer which decides its own path once the target is set in it, so that firing aircraft does not have to wait until the target is struck. This makes pilot less vulnerable to enemy fire and also have increased accuracy.

Reactive Armour (ERA) on the latest tank. It will home in on the target from the top, which is the most vulnerable part of a tank. It is capable of being fired at night.

Nag

The other two are **nuclear capable ballistic missiles**.

Prithvi

Prithvi is single stage liquid fuel missile. It comes in category of Short Range Ballistic Missile (SRBM). Its range is 250 kilometer with 500 kg warhead and 150 kilometer with 1000 kg warhead. 8.5 metre long missile with latest on-board computer and an advanced inertial navigation system is capable of carrying warheads. It can use both solid and liquid propellants. It can be fired from a mobile launcher and takes just 5 minutes to reach its target at a distance of 150 kilometer. India has about 100 Prithvi launchers. Though it has strike Aircrafts which outperform Prithvi-II, as it is named, in terms of range, accuracy and weapon load, but defence sources say, "*Prithvi-II has a definite role in circumstances when strike Aircraft cannot fly, but one needs to keep the pressure up.*"

Agni

The first trial of the short range variation of the nuclear capable Agni missile was conducted on January 25, 2001. The 15 metre tall, 1 metre diameter and 12 ton single-stage missile is powered by solid fuel propulsion. It is surface-to-surface missile capable of striking targets up to a distance of 700 kilometer. It can be fired from a mobile launcher. Its launch would help in evaluating the performance of certain critical technologies like guidance and telemetry systems. DRDO officials say that the Pakistan specific shorter range Agni variant is a bridge between Prithvi-II (250 kilometer range) and Agni-II (which can strike targets 2500 km away). It is a guided missile and is designed to carry a nuclear warhead. India has, at present, 20 Agni missiles.

As mentioned earlier Agni-II is 2500 km IRBM and comprises two stages, one is the same as solid fuel Agni-I and the second stage is liquid fuel Prithvi. It is capable of targeting some Chinese cities. Efforts are on to convert 150 to 3000 kg payload Space Launch Vehicle (SLV) into an ICBM. For this the necessary guidance system, weapon explosives and other spares are already available. This will probably be named as Agni-III.

Agni-III

Nuclear Triad: India's naval chief Admiral Madhvendra Singh said, "India being a declared nuclear state with no-first-use doctrine, must have a Nuclear Triad with country's strongest nuclear weapon platform to be under sea." This is essential as land based nuclear weapons could be targeted. The acquisition of a nuclear submarine will herald the arrival of India as a genuine nuclear weapon power. So India is seeking a nuclear-propelled submarine, which can operate under the sea for long periods of time without replenishment. It is looking at two Russian Shchuka Bar Class nuclear propelled SSBN submarines capable of launching ballistic and cruise missiles, thereby providing India with the third crucial leg of the nuclear triad.

India and Russia are already jointly developing the 300 kilometer BrahMos supersonic cruise missile which can be launched from a submarine.

The Table 5.2 gives the list of missiles currently in India's inventory or under development that can carry Nuclear Warheads.

Table 5.2. India's Nuclear- Capable Missiles

Name	*Class*	*Range (km)*	*Payload*	*Status (kg)*
Akash	SAM	30	60	Operational
Sagarika	SLBM	700-2,200	150-1,000	Under development
Shaurya	TBM	700-2,200	150-1,000	Under development
Agni-I	SRBM	700	1000	Operational
Agni-II	MRBM	2,200	500-1,000	Operational
Agni-II Prime	MRBM	2,750-3,000	500-1,500	Under development
Agni-III	IRBM	3,500	2,490	Under induction
Agni-V (Surya)	ICBM	5,000-6,000	3,000	Under development
Agni 3SL	ICBM	5,200-11,600	700-1,400	Under development
Dhanush	SRBM	350	500	Operational
Prithvi-I	SRBM	150	1,000	Operational
Prithvi-II	SRBM	250	500	Operational
Prithvi-III	SRBM	350	500	Operational
Cruise Missiles				
Nirbhay	Subsonic	1,000	–	Under development
BrahMos	Supersonic	290	300	Operational
P-70 Ametist	Anti-shipping	65	530	Operational
P-270 Moskit	Supersonic	120	320	Operational
Popeye	ASM	78	340	Operational

Dhanush Missile

Agni-V: Nuclear Capable ICBM. Also Named Surya

Indian Ballistic Missile Defence Program (IBMDP): As described earlier, Ballistic missiles, using a ballistic trajectory usually deliver a warhead over the horizon. India has an active ABM development effort using indigenously developed and integrated radars and locally designed missiles. In November 2006, India successfully conducted the Prithvi Air Defence Exercise (PADE) in which anti-ballistic missile, called the Prithvi Air Defence (PAD) an Exo-atmospheric (outside atmosphere) Interceptor System intercepted a Prithvi-II ballistic missile. The PAD missile has the secondary stage of the Prithvi missile and can reach altitude of 80 kilometer. During the test the target missile was intercepted at an 50 kilometer altitude. India became the fourth nation in the world to acquire such a capability and the third nation to develop it through indigenous efforts.

On December 6, 2007 the AAD missile system was tested successfully. The missile is an Endo-atmospheric interceptor with the altitude of 30 kilometers. The missile ensures a hit probability of 99.8 percent. Two new high speed anti-ballistic missiles AD-1 and AD-2 that can intercept IRBM/ICBM with the range of 5000 kilometers are being developed.

India has Russian S300 PMU-2, which is used as an interceptor for ballistic missiles. An indigenous nuclear tipped surface-to-air missile Akash is used to destroy low range missile and is capable of destroying various targets and is one of few of its kind systems in the world.

Cruise Missiles: *We know that a cruise missile is a jet engine or rocket-propelled missile that flies at low altitude using an automated guidance system to make them hard to detect or intercept*. As given in Table 5.2, India has a number of cruise missiles. Their detailed description is given below.

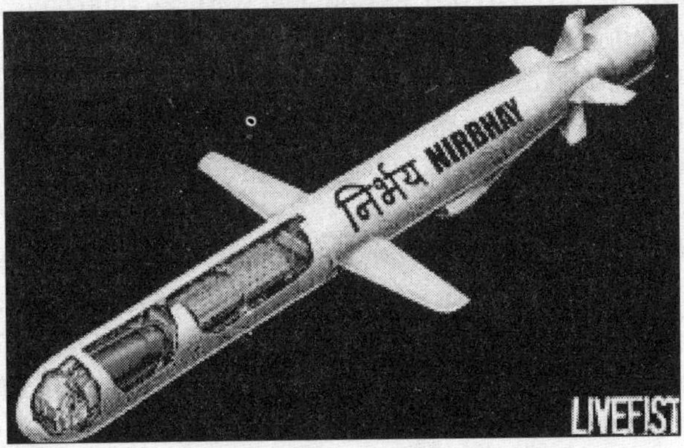

Nirbhay-Supersonic Cruise Missile

Nirbhay: It is a long range subsonic cruise missile being developed in India. Its range will be 1,000 kilometers and will arm three services Army, Navy and Air Force. It will be able to be launched from multiple platforms on land, sea and air. Nirbhay will be a terrain hugging , stealth missile capable of delivering 24 different types of warheads depending on mission requirements and will use inertial navigation system for guidance.

3M-54 Klub: The Russian Klub is a multi-role missile system with a range of 250-300 kilometer and an average speed of 0.8 Mach* with a maximum of 2.9 Mach. India has acquired about 200 such missiles for arming Talwar class frigate, Shivalik class frigate, Kolkata class destroyer and Sindhughosh class submarine. Due to Klub's longer range than BrahMos, it may also be used in the Mirage 2,000 and Su-30 MKI.

Popeye: In 1999, India imported a large number of Israel Rafael made Popeye missiles. Popeye-II, an air-launched nuclear capable cruise missile with a range of 80 kilometers can be launched from planes, was given to India along with missile defence radars in a deal. 20-50 missiles could have been given with possibly more being built in India. The planes to be armed with these missiles are thought to be Tu-142, Sukhoi Su-30 MKI.

P-70 Ametist: India has these Soviet, submarine-launched cruise missiles which can carry nuclear warheads and have a range of 50-65 kilometers.

P-270 Moskit: India has a number of these Russian, supersonic ramjet powered cruise missiles capable of being launched from land and ships. Moskits, with a range of 120 kilometer have been kept in reserve but can be used.

BrahMos: It is a supersonic cruise missile that can be launched from land, aircraft, ship or submarine. It is the product of 'BrahMos Aerospace Private Limited', a joint venture of India's DRDO and Russia's NPO Mashinostroeyenia. The acronnym BrahMos is perceived as the confluence of two great rivers—India's **Brahmputra** and Russia's **Moskva**.

---

* It is a unitless quantity. That is, it is number giving the ratio of the air speed of an aircraft to the velocity of sound under given conditions.

Although BrahMos is primarily an anti-ship missile, it can also engage land based targets. It can be launched either in a vertical or inclined position and is capable of covering targets over 360 degree horizon. BrahMos has an identical configuration for land, sea and sub-sea platforms. The air-launched version has a smaller booster and additional tail fins for added stability during launch.

Brahmos travels at speeds of Mach 2.5 to 2.8 and is the world's fastest cruise missile—three and a half times as fast as the USA's subsonic Harpoon cruise missile. A hypersonic version of the missile is also presently under development. (lab tested with 5.26 Mach speed). BrahMos claims to have the capability of attacking surface targets as low as 10 meter in altitude. It has a maximum range of 290 kilometers. The ship launched and land-based missiles can carry a 200 kilogram warhead, where-as the aircraft-launched variant (BrahMos A) can carry a 300 kilogram warhead. It has two-stage propulsion system, with a solid- propellant rocket for initial acceleration and a liquid-fueled ramjet responsible for sustained supersonic cruise.

Brahmos

The BrahMos is currently being configured for aerial deployment with the Su-30 MKI as its carrier.

Delivery Mechanism:

Nuclear Submarines: Indian plans are to have 20 nuclear submarines capable of carrying missiles with nuclear warheads. Currently, India has built one and is building two more nuclear submarines under the Advanced Technology Vessel (ATV) plan. India currently maintains six submarines of the ***Sindhughosh class*** that can launch the nuclear capable 3M-54 Klub cruise missiles.

Arihant Class Submarines: These submarines are a class of

India's Nuclear Powered, Arihant Class of Submarine

Scorpene Class Submarine

nuclear-powered ballistic missile submarines being constructed at Visakhapatnam for the Indian navy under the ATV project. The ATV is an SSBN and will be armed with ballistic missiles.

The first of these, INS Arihant was launched on July 26, 2009. The vessel which will undergo sea-trials for up to two years, will then be equipped with an unknown number of K-15 Sagarika SLBMs. The second and third submarines of this class may incorporate the Nirbhay as well. As of July, 2007, the Sagarika missiles as well as Dhanush had undergone three successful tests each.

INS Cruise Missile Submarines: The INS Sindhuraj, INS Sindhuvir, INS Sindhuratna, INS Sindhushastra, INS Sindhukesari and INS Sindhuvijay are capable of launching 3M-54 Klub and BrahMos nuclear capable cruise missiles.

Akula and Amur Submarines: In 2000, India went for a deal with Russia to rent two Akula class submarines. The defence experts say that the so called lease agreement would be eventually modified and India would keep the submarines. The first submarine will be named INS Chakra.

Russia has also offered the advanced Amur class submarines, known as S1000. According to Global Security India is already building the S1000 cruise missile submarines in Mazagaon docks. The Amur will most probably be fitted with P-700 Granit or the Klub cruise missile capable of carrying nuclear warheads.

Frigates, Destroyers and Aircraft Carriers: India also maintains ships such as destroyers, modified petrol crafts and frigates which can launch nuclear capable ballistic and cruise missiles.

Frigates such as Talwar class and Shivalik class can fire nuclear capable cruise missiles. The variations of these two frigates are prepared so as to suit for launching supersonic nuclear 3M-54 Klub cruise missiles, BrahMos, barak or SAMs and Harbour helicopters such as HAL Dhruv or Nirbhay missiles.

Talwar Class Frigate

Destroyers with Indian Navy such as Rajput-class, Kolkata-class and Delhi-class may be armed with nuclear capable missiles Nirbhay or even 3M-54 Klub cruise missiles.

The ship-launched Dhanush ballistic missile was tested from INS Subhadra of the Sukanya class *petrol craft* in 2,000. INS Subhadra is patrol vessel which was modified and the missile was launched from the re-enforced helicopter deck. In 2004, the missile was tested successfully from the Subhadra.

Aircraft carrier INS Vikramaditya was fitted with P-500 Bazalt nuclear capable cruise missile of the range 550 kilometer. India is also a potential customer for a Slava class cruiser which also incorporates the P-500 Bazalt.

Nuclear-Capable Aircrafts: India currently has *forth generation* jet fighters capable of launching nuclear weapons. Such aircrafts are also seen as a less expensive way of dropping nuclear warheads as well as being as effective.

Sukhoi Su-30

Fighter Jets: The Sukhoi Su-30 MKI, Dassault Mirage 2,000 and MiG-29 serve in the Indian Air Force and are also seen as a means to deliver nuclear weapons. In addition, India maintains SEPECAT Jaguar and MiG-27M which can be used to drop gravity bombs. On the other hand, the Su-30 MKI, capable of carrying nuclear weapons and tailor-made for Indian specifications, integrates Indian systems and avionics, is one of the best air superiority fighters and also consists of French and Israeli subsystems. The Mirage 2000Hs were heavily customised during the Kargil War and is the only other version , other than the French 2000N to be able to be armed with nuclear weapons. MiG-29 like the HAL Tejas has the capacity to be armed with nuclear weapons. Both HAL Tejas and Su-30 MKI can travel excess of 3,000 kilometers without refueling. This allows India to attack targets far away in the effective manner only using planes rather than delivery systems such as Agni.

The ***HAL Tejas*** is India's only indigenous plane to be armed with nuclear weapons, thus making India less dependent on Russia.

India has leased four Russian Tupolev Tu-22M3 bombers, which could carry air-launched cruise missiles. India has upgraded

Tejas

its Russian-built Tu-142 maritime petrol aircraft to carry air-launched cruise missiles. India is also considering buying Sukhoi T-50 stealth fighter jets from Russia.

Few More Achievements: The technological achievement demonstrated by Pokhran tests is certainly an act to be proud of. In the post-Pokhran-II scenario, India has emerged as the first country—even ahead of the US and Russia—to build thermonuclear weapons with variable charges. In other words, India is now in a position to arm its missiles with multipurpose warheads capable of fulfilling tactical as well as strategic tasks.

Another wonder has been done by India's technical and engineering staff in the Rajasthan desert that is, the repair and overhaul of the Rajasthan nuclear power station and bring it on steam through completely indigenous technology and efforts at a fraction of the cost in other countries.

Production of Tritium: Moreover India has achieved the technology to produce the highly unstable radioactive substance Tritium—which is so vital for nuclear weapon loads—from heavy water. This will enable the country to mass produce Tritium in no time at all—an accomplishment which lends a powerful new definition to the Indian nuclear program.

Param-1000: In March,1998, Indian Scientists from centre for Advance Computing, C-DEC at Pune developed indigenously a giga-flop Super Computer 'Param 1000' capable of doing 100 billion arithmetic computations per second. This capacity can be made ten fold by adopting parallel combinations. It is believed that a computer with a capacity of doing one trillion computations per second (terra flop) is available only with America, Japan and India. These super computers are used in simulations of gigantic systems like cosmos. These are also being used to simulate the micro systems of the atomic level. So these are extremely helpful in making nuclear bombs of various designs and power, specially the small bombs called low-yield or sub-kiloton bombs indigenous technology and efforts at a fraction of the cost in other countries.

Security Systems: Similarly, India as nation is proud of developing systems to fight nuclear exposure. After Russia, China, Israel and some NATO countries, India also has joined the select band of military powers by indigenously developing protective system which not only combats contamination caused by nuclear, biological and chemical weapons but also functions as a nuclear shelter. The DRDO has designed and developed this Nuclear, Biological and Chemical (NBC) system. The NBC system can effectively work in a contaminated area and remove the deadly effects of nuclear weapons. According to Rajiv Nayan of the Institute of Defence studies and Analysis (IDSA), the NBC systems were the need of the hour. We know, the deadly radiations, coupled with release of extreme heat, and rise in air pressure due to the blast of (say) 20 kiloton nuclear bomb can prevent entry of any man or vehicle within a radius of 1.5 kilometer. The NBC system works from a distance facilitating the soldiers' entry to the contaminated area to carry out decontamination process. For protection against biological arms, special systems have been evolved which can guard respiratory tracts and filter the contaminated air besides immunising the troops against disease causing organism. There is also a system to combat chemical weapons effectively by clearing a contaminated zone of toxic chemicals, at the same time the system can prevent entry of harmful materials through the skin or by inhalation.

***The NBC Collective Protective System* (*CPS*)** can provide protection even against a nuclear blast. The CPS is a pre-fabricated galvanised steel structure with two main living modules that can shelter 60 people for 96 hours and a utility module all connected by vestibules. The structure also comprises an entry, an exit and a decontamination unit. Always kept one metre under the ground, the whole system can be dug up, the components assembled and the system made functional within about 15 hours. The system can be used at a command post, observation post or for storage of medical supplies, fuel and food in a contaminated area. The CPS has built in filters to provide fresh air free from contamination. The supply of fresh air is managed by maintaining pressure inside the unit higher than the outside atmospheric pressure. Hence the contaminated air cannot enter inside. Allied equipment includes a generator set, a filtration/ventilation system, water storage facilities and waste disposal system.

India's Security concerns: India has two immediate threats—from Pakistan and China.

Pakistan: Initially Pakistan was considered to be having 15 to 25 primitive nuclear bombs. These first generation nuclear bombs, because of their technical limitations were relatively big in weight and size and require large and powerful delivery systems even to carry them over relatively small distances. Apart from this, Pakistan has F-16 and Mirage-3 fighter bombers. It has 80 kilometer range Hatfa-1 and 300 kilometer range Hatfa-2 missiles. Its M-11 missile can also strike up to 300 kilometer. It has IRBMs Ghauri and Gazanavi with range of 1500 kilometer and 2000 kilometer respectively.

But 2011 estimates reveal that the current stockpile with Pakistan is 100-110 warheads. According to a US congressional report, Pakistan has built hard and deeply buried storage and launch facilities to retain a second strike capability in case of nuclear war.

It is confirmed that Pakistan had built Soviet-style road mobile missiles, state-of-the-art air defences around strategic sites, and other concealment measures.

Pakistani engineers, with the help from the Chinese, are also said to be in the advanced stage of developing MIRV technology for its missiles. This would allow the military to fit several warheads on the same ballistic missile and then launch them at separate targets.

Pakistan Air Force (PAF) is believed to have practiced 'Toss bombing' in the 1990s, a method of launching weapons from fighter bombers which can also be used to deliver nuclear weapons. PAF has two units (Number 16 Squadron and Number 26 Squadron) operating around 50 of the Chinese-built Nanchang A-5c, believed to be the preferred vehicle for the delivery of nuclear weapons due to its long range. The others are various variants of the Dassault Mirage-III and Dassault Mirage-V, of which around 156 are currently operated by PAF. The PAF also operates some 63 F-16 fighters, the first 32 of which were delivered in 1980s and believed to have been modified for nuclear weapon delivery.

An Air-launched cruise missile (ALCM) with range of 350 kilometer has been developed by Pakistan, designated as Hatfa-8 and named Ra'ad ALCM which may theoretically be armed with nuclear warhead.

An expert opinion is that the flight duration of missiles fired by Pakistan on just one Indian city, Mumbai, is as little as three minutes and that would kill between 150,000 and 850,000 people.

But, Pakistan even with this might is capable to do a limited attack on Indian targets. Therefore, Indian program which results in the possession of few similar bombs and missiles will be adequate.

China: On the other hand, we must be capable of a more graduated response against China. China is a Super Power and has the full equipment of nuclear weapons and delivery systems. China is considered to have more than 400 warheads deployed on land and submarine based missiles and nuclear capable bombers. It possesses two types of ICBMs with the range 7,000 and 11,000 kilometer. These are fitted with 2 and 5 Megaton warheads. Its DF-3 IRBMs can strike over a range of 3,000 kilometer with 2 megaton warhead and DF-21 missile with 200 to 300 kiloton warhead can strike a target up to 1,800 kilometer. Out of these only DF-3 missile is capable of attacking India. China has 86 IRBM and 27 ICBM launchers. In addition to this it also has 120 TU-16 bomber planes with 3,100 kilometer range. It is pursuing its—largest by any nation—nuclear and missile expansion.

Like other major powers, China is investing in the area of sea-based deterrent—invulnerable Submarine Launched Ballistic Missile (SLBM). It has 12 submarines each equipped with ballistic missiles, capable of carrying a 2 megaton warhead and strike up to 2,700 kilometer. China is moving towards putting multiple nuclear warheads on each of its next generation strategic missiles and developing at least four 'Project 094' nuclear submarines by 2010. This modernization program and related nuclear missilery is estimated to be relevant till 2070 A.D. So a massive Chinese conventional attack or a limited nuclear strike with tactical weapons cannot be deterred by counter-value weapons. The small tactical weapons with accurate delivery systems will be a far more credible deterrent.

China's nuclear posture is also beginning to acquire a new assertive tenor. It has already modified its *'no-first-use' (NFU)* posture. In 1995, it dropped the word 'unconditional' from its pledge and added the condition of excluding India—membership in the NPT and a nuclear weapon free zone. At the same time, it refuses to foreswear covert technology transfer to Pakistan. Such state-sponsored proliferation to a state-sponsor of terrorism has been complicated by the US military presence in Pakistan. Even so, secret pacts on unspecified military cooperation were signed in March, 2002 during a flying visit to Islamabad by general Xiang Guangkai of China. Indications are that the Chinese leadership still values horizontal proliferation as an indispensable component of balance of power politics and an instrument of leverage to win US concessions.

China is all set for formally moving from *minimum to limited deterrence or from counter-value to counterforce* targeting. China is pursuing a three-tiered posture; one, credible minimum deterrence against America and Russia; two, limited deterrence around its other periphery; and three, offensively configured counterforce strategy with even pre-emption, for the conventionally armed missile forces of its second artillery. The second and third modes are of direct significance to India which is presently working to militarily integrate its nuclear weapons and develop new Intermediate range delivery systems.

The US and Russia: At present, India has no threat from the two super powers US and Russia. But defence experts opine that we must not judge others by their motivations but by their capabilities. These two countries have tremendous conventional capabilities in the vicinity of India. Both have bases in the Indian Ocean in Diego Garcea and Socotra respectively. The US seventh fleet with its awesome fire power is always nearby. The US can also launch long range bombers like B-52 and B-1 from Diego Garcea.

The new *US Nuclear Posture Review* (NPR) report has revealed two US initiatives: the setting up of 'Advanced Warhead Concept' teams, and a feasibility study into developing a nuclear earth-borrowing warhead. A new ICBM, SLBM, SSBN and heavy bomber—all armed with novel nuclear warheads—are planned for deployment between the years 2020-2040. Using an innovating concept, '*operationally deployed*', US intends to pursue an illusory arms cut—reducing its active warheads from over 12000 to 2200 within 10 years, but keeping the surplus weapons in a way to reactivate them at quick notice. The NPR has also revealed America's contingency plans for use of nuclear weapons against at least seven nations—China, Russia, North Korea, Iran, Iraq, Libya and Syria.

A blue-water Indian Navy is certainly not a credible answer to this. India has to upgrade its technological and defence development program much beyond what it is contemplating now. Howsoever irrational the possession of nuclear weapons may seem, there is a certain rationality that applies once that threshold is crossed. Not to obey that rationality would open a country to much greater risk than before.

Brahma Chellaney, a defence analyst says, "One of the wisest decisions India took since independence was to go overtly nuclear. That overdue decision has helped raise India's International stature, aid its security interests, and anchor its policy in pragmatism". India has wisely increased its strategic space in Asia by developing close ties both with the US and Russia. China is actively conscious of India's diplomatic level and strategic opportunity. The nuclear equilibrium has stabilised relations between and among the warring nation-states of Europe which had been turned into a slaughterhouse of the world twice in 20 years. India's nuclear bomb will also restore balance in South Asia as it did in Europe.

The NPR plans are no threat to Indian security. If anything, India's challenge is to draw what the NPR lists as the benefits of reliable nuclear weapons: assures allies and friends, dissuade competitors, deter aggressors and defeat enemies.

How Much Nuclear India Needs? "*More is not better if less is enough for nuclear deterrent*", says General K. Sunderji, India's former Army Chief. Objectively speaking India has only a minimum nuclear deterrent that is not enough to face the dangerous nuclear environment around it. It has yet to establish a credible deterrent. In purely military terms, the country is capable of designing a complete range of nuclear warheads of different intensity which can be fitted on missiles, mounting on deep penetrating strike aircrafts or possibly launched at sea. The last option is not currently available to India. Prithvi, 150-300 kilometer range surface-to-surface missile and 2,500 kilometer range Agni delivery system—which can carry a thermonuclear warhead—cannot cover the whole of China, it can only deter an adventurist Pakistan. The two sub-kiloton tests conducted for weapon calibration is obviously a step to miniaturize the nuclear warhead for fitting it on a missile. We need to apply our technology to manufacture nuclear weapons of various hues.

As any nuclear weapon program must go hand in hand with manufacture of delivery systems, India has to develop ICBM or a long range missile. India's GSLV rocket technology is no different from that applied for manufacturing ICBMs, yet India is a step away from perfecting the re-entry of the trajectory and the guidance system. It means we have to develop engineering acumen to guide the missile towards a specific target. We know in case of actual nuclear conflict it is the second strike capability that matters. That is, we must be able to sustain the offensive even after loosing launching platforms in retaliatory strikes by the enemy. Therefore, we need to develop sea-launch facilities which are still on the drawing board stage. Answer to this problem lies in India's Sagarika cruise missile program which belongs to the field of submarine launched missiles. So we need nuclear powered submarines.

Against this background, the government should avoid participating in the negotiations for the conclusion of Fissile Material Cut-off Treaty (FMCT) in the impending Geneva-based conference on Disarmament. Without Fissile material at its disposal, India cannot hope to consummate its nuclear prowess. With the expected sanctions, India cannot import the dual use technology and the same would have to be developed by Indian scientists.

Cost of Nuclear Weaponisation of India: Some persons from India and outside think that if India goes for nuclear weaponisation its economy will be destroyed. Actually when they say this, their estimates are associated with the massive cost spent by the US and Russia on their nuclear arsenals which comprises tens of thousands of warheads deployed globally. China paid about $4 billion for its somewhat smaller force numbering about 400 warheads. This amount of course, does not include the cost of missile program which came later. Manoj Joshi of 'India Today' who frequently writes on subjects of nuclear technology has different but realistic views. Quoting many authorities on nuclear weaponisation costing, he emphasizes that inducting nuclear warheads will have negligible impact on defence spending provided India sticks to the policy of minimum deterrent posture. This is because security does not come from more numbers. China has 14 missiles aimed at the US and the US has 1400 missiles aimed at China. Even then deterrence works.

According to India's former Air Chief Marshal N.C. Suri, After these five tests (in May, 1998) we have been able to generate enough data which will help us do computer simulations, we do not really need a massive weapons program. You just need to satisfy your weapon program according to the threats that are manifest. The defence analyst G. Balachandran writes that the nuclear weaponisation will raise the country's present annual spending of Rs. 40,000 crore on defence related activities by only 3 per cent. This spending is the lowest percentage of the GDP of many countries such as Israel, China, Japan, Iran and even Pakistan. The defence expenditure could be further reduced if the defence ministry structures the way the armed forces are organised and equipped in the light of induction of weapons of mass destruction in the armoury.

The reason for the low cost of the Indian program is that many of the facilities and institutions like BARC required for a credible deterrent force have already been set up over the past decades. The waste from the reactors like Dhruv is processed to yield the weapon grade Plutonium. Agni's first stage is nothing but SLV-3 rocket which is a part of India's civilian space program. We already have "***Param-1000***" a gigaflop super computer required for designing new nuclear bombs with simulation techniques. Very recently, in 2003, BARC has developed country's most efficient computer ***Anupam-PIB-64***. It is three times faster than its earlier super computer and 1000 time faster the first one. According to P.K. Ayenger, former AEC Chairman, only 2 per cent of the manpower from BARC has been used in the bomb activity. He also estimates the cost of each warhead to be less than one crore and not 4 crores as estimated by General K. Sunderji in 1996.

As already mentioned in the opinion of General Sunderji, the *more is not better if less is enough for nuclear deterrence.* Therefore, the Indian opinion is to adopt a minimum deterrent posture. Considering the opinion of various experts in the field of nuclear weapon technology and military, one can suggest that India's stock of nuclear war arsenal should comprise of ***20 Prithvi missiles, 20 Agni missiles, 60 nuclear warheads and 5 nuclear submarines.*** Apart from this India must have a command control system, satellite surveillance and targeting system and also rail-base system. Experts price the first four items at Rs. 8 crore, 20 crore, 1 crore and 4000 crore each respectively. The cost of the remaining three systems is estimated to be Rs. 2000 crore, 2500 crore and 500 crore respectively. If this program is spread over 10 years, the total cost amounts to be Rs. 25,620 crore. As already suggested, this cost is not unaffordable by a country like India.

If the country moves fast in reformulating the defence strategy and structuring it in the light of India's overt nuclear weapon capacity, and reduces the cost of sprawling and inefficient military-industrial complex by ridding it of excess manpower, inefficient ordinance factories and establishment, we can get, as it is said, the biggest bang for our limited bucks.

Nuclear Command Authority of India: It was nearly five years since India declared itself *a Nuclear Weapon Power* following the Pokhran tests in 1998. But no formal Command and Control Structure was set up. There was a loosely knit structure in operation, but the need for formalising it and making it public became imperative in recent months, especially after 10 month long military stand-off with Pakistan which threatened to take on a nuclear dimension. If confusion prevails in respect of rules regarding use of weapons and delivery systems, a panic reaction in an emergency can set off untold consequences. Therefore, the Cabinet Committee on Security (CCS), in its meeting on January 4, 2003 adopted and made public the key elements of its nuclear doctrine and command structure.

The Doctrine: *A nuclear strike could be ordered if India and its forces anywhere in the world were attacked with weapons of mass destruction, including nuclear, chemical and biological ones.*

It should be noted that the Doctrine includes the eventuality of its troops in a conventional war being attacked by chemical or biological weapons. This became necessary since India, being a signatory to the Chemical and Biological Weapon Convention, does not possess such weapons.

The Command Structure: The Nuclear Command Authority (NCA) would have at the apex a civilian Political Council chaired by the Prime Minister. The NCA structure has three components.

1. **The Political Council (PC):** Chaired by the Prime Minister Atal Behari Vajpayee, the council will include Deputy Prime Minister Lal Krishna Advani, Defence Minister George Fernandes, Foreign Minister Yashwant Sinha and Finance Minister Jaswant Singh. PM's Principal Secretary and Cabinet Secretary will also be present. A retaliatory nuclear attack can only be authorised by this civilian council. As the first among equals, the Prime Minister will symbolically have his finger on the Nuclear button.
2. **The Executive Council (EC):** This council will be chaired by PM's Principal Secretary, Brajesh Mishra, who is also the National Security Advisor. The Cabinet Secretary, DRDO Chief V.K. Aatre, AEC chairman Anil Kakodkar, The three service chiefs through 'Chiefs of Staff Committee' headed by Admiral Madhavendra Singh are members. The council will provide inputs for decision-making to the NCA and execute directions given by PC. DRDO builds the delivery systems and AEC makes the core to equip with vital technological information required for decision making. The Chiefs of Staff Committee would ensure that the orders are carried out in case of strike.

3. **The Strategic Force Command (SFC):** This tri-service command under a Commander-in-Chief will be the custodian of all nuclear weapons and delivery systems. It will, in case of a nuclear attack, will formulate the strategy for retaliation, that is, it would work out plans and targets, and also the number of nuclear weapons required to form a 'minimum credible deterrence', and it will advise the Chiefs of Staff committee to actually fire the nukes.

National Command Authority of India

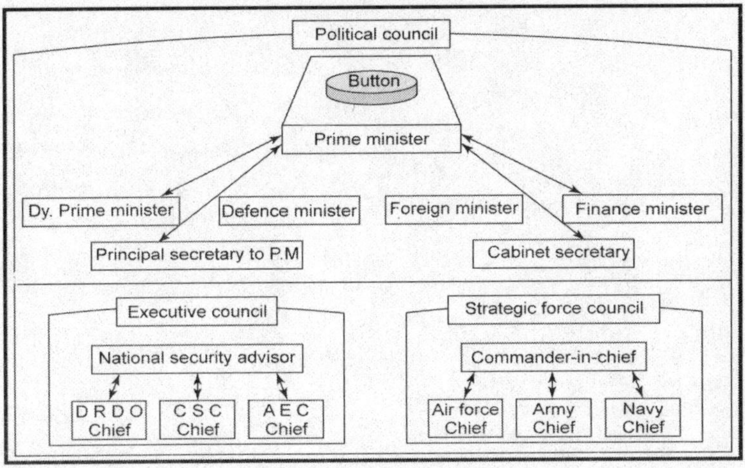

A clear step-by-step plan has been devised to eliminate any chances of a mischievous or accidental detonation of nuclear weapons. While the armed forces have operational control at the SFC level, DRDO scientists will be involved in the making of the warheads with the missiles and AEC scientists will be in-charge of the core. This will minimise misuse and make the system failsafe and foolproof.

According to CCS announcement, Prime Minister will be the sole authority to order a nuclear strike. But our present system of electing PM is a matter of several steps, even an incumbent may suddenly be incapacitated in the event of a nuclear attack or otherwise. To tackle such a serious situation alternative chain of command has also been approved as a back up to the main one. But it has not been made public because of secrecy reasons.

One problem is yet to be tackled. If non-state actors, such as terrorists or terrorists instigated by state actors attack the country with nuclear, chemical or biological weapons, India does not have any safety arrangement in such situations.

❑

6

When Buddha Smiles

> ***"Perfect peace would never come until all the nations of the earth were equally mighty."***
>
> ***— Bhagwan Gautam Buddha.***

May be apparently ironic but befitting code names, '*The Smiling Buddha*' and 'Shakti' were selected for Pokhran-I and Pokhran-II explosions respectively. On the 1974 explosion we said *Buddha Smiles* and on 1998 explosions we said *Buddha smiled again,* for both these operations were enacted on *Buddha Purnima*, the day Gautam, the apostle of peace attained *Nirvana*. In the case of May 18, 1974 when India performed a peaceful nuclear explosion (pne), the code was not chosen at random. Perhaps, Dr. Raja Ramanna, the man behind Pokhran 1974 or Smt. Indira Gandhi, the then Prime Minister, remembered that 25 centuries back Buddha, the supreme realist, advocated for a mighty nation and pleaded against unilateral disarmament. The following quote is relevant to Buddha's comments over a war:

"Once Magadh king Ajatshatru attacked the Lichhavi confederacy led by Vaishali and killed mercilessly the peace-loving but brave people of the land of famous patriot and dancer Amrapaali. When Buddha heard of it he was dismayed that his disciples of Magadh should have attacked his Sakya kinsmen. He sighed and said, "***Perfect peace would never come until all the nations of the earth were equally mighty***."

In case of *Shakti* (meaning Strength and also the name of Goddess of Strength), the team at work maintains that the date of the tests, May 11, was not deliberately chosen to coincide with Buddha Purnima. The scientists were ready to test a week earlier, but held back for a simple reason: President K.R. Narayanan was out of country and was to return on May 10. It looked odd to carry out such tests when the head of State was on a foreign tour. One can say, if one believes, that Brahma himself has destined the Pokhran-II again on Buddha Purnima, that is, May 11, 1998. It should be reminded that according to astrologers like Ajay Bhambi, the planetary conditions when these tests were performed, that is, at 3:45 PM on May 11 and at 12:21PM on May 13 of the year 1998, and May 18, 1974 were more or less same.

Today, some thought it ironic that the Enlightened One's name was linked to weaponry. He himself, being a supreme realist, never preached unilateral disarmament. Incidentally, it is relevant to note that much the same point was made in the wake of Pokhran-II by the representatives of two leading Buddhist nations—the Dalai Lama and the foreign Minister of Sri Lanka.

Actually, the wealth of atomic weapons *(Brahamastras)* is the ancient brave tradition of this land of Buddha. India's all Great warriors, Rama, Arjun, Karan, Dronacharya, Bhishma, Parshuram et al. possessed Brahmastra. It cannot be a mere coincidence that most of the Brahmastras were built by Lord Shiva who lived and experimented on Himalayas, which even now, has the richest Uranium deposits. None of the Indian gods is seen without a weapon in his/her hands. Even Santoshi Mata is endowed with a Trishul and Sword. No brave nation can be afraid of weapons. The Sword, Dhanush (Arch), Trishul etc. are the traditional toys which the Indian children play with.

But a brave nation like India, because of its background of *Vedanta Philosophy* can never cause destruction. *India is the only nation able to go nuclear but choosing not to do so for 24 years till it was compelled by the countries surrounding it, indulged in nuclear weapon activities.* This is a manifestation of India's unique strategic culture that is wedded to global disarmament even while grappling with the dictates of realism and real politik in a vitiated regional environment. Look at India's glorious history of more than 5,000 years. None of its heroes used his might to crush the feelings of their detractors or to enslave others. They always used their might to establish peace and to behead the Demons. The aim is '*World Brotherhood*' ("वसुधैव कुटुम्बकम्") and the guiding principle is as Lord Krishna declared in Gita:

परित्रणाय साधूनां विनाय च दुकृताम्।
धर्म संस्थपनार्थाय संभवामि युगे-युगे॥

(I appear again and again to protect gentlemen, to destroy wicked men and to establish the rule of law).

We should remember that after visiting the ground zero of Pokhran 1998 explosions, the Prime Minister Atal Behari Vajpayee made it clear, "*India wants peace in the world and it also believes that science is for protection and not for destruction; it should be utilised for development and not for creating trouble. I want to assure that we will proceed in the constructive direction of science.*"

One should remember that the man who pushed for nuclear weaponisation of India is Dr. A.P.J. Abdul Kalam, who in India's best secular traditions reads Gita, prays at the Rameshwaram Temple and plays Rudra Veena. The Smile of Lord Buddha on both the occasions radiates the message that our nuclear weapons are not meant for destruction; they are only to maintain peace in the world.

Those who Joined the Smiling Buddha: Those who loved India and wanted it to rise, felt elevated on Pokhran blasts. Pokhran explosions blew the trumpet of national pride and Indians felt the depth of national security. Pokhran has raised the self confidence of the Indian people and brightened the faces of the Indian lovers abroad. Indians hope their nukes will both blow away any doubts about India's role as a great power, and end its long, painful inferiority complex towards sneering westerners, and rampant neighbours in the Northern and Western borders. Indians will finally get respect. As in 1974, the nuclear tests gave the nation a pleasant and proud surprise, this time the news thrilled the nation. There was euphoria and joy. On other occasions, the lifting of drooping spirits was pulpable.

Bobby John Varkey writes in *Hindustan Times* Sunday Magazine: Anywhere in Rajasthan, you find everybody talking of nothing but India's tryst of a different kind. They all know that their land has been catapulated into international fame and are eager to share the proud moment as their own. Right from Hissar in Haryana to Bikaner, from shopkeepers to restaurant owners, everybody calls the achievement as their own. An old villager says, "If Pakistan has Ghaury missile, it is good that they know, we have something even bigger." To the surprise of Journalists, people in the remotest villages, all know what the explosion was all about. A villager 4 kilometer from the test site says, "*Ab hamare desh ki shakti bhi badh gayi hai.*"

The same was the experience of former foreign secretary, Shri J.N. Dixit who happened to be in Jodhpur on May 12 and 13:

There was dancing in the streets, fire works and distribution of sweets by ordinary people in the rural areas. One of the locals distributing the sweets said when asked about his feeling, "***Sar ooncha karke chalenge ab yeh bhi bata diya dunia ko ki akal hai aur haath me kaarigari hai.***"

The Hindustan Times wrote in its front page special editorial captioned '*A Moment of Pride*', 'the smiling Buddha of 1974 has now blossomed into a new assertion of the country's right to arm itself in a manner which, it believes, is best suited to its security interests. It goes without saying that for all the appeals of the existing nuclear powers to threshold countries to desist from testing these *doomsday* weapons, India could not have ignored that it happens to be part of a hostile environment where benign pecifism is not only unfeasible but may even send the wrong message of weakness to countries which have desire to live in friendship,....'

It was 3:44 PM when the Prime Minister, Shri Atal Behari Vajpayee along with his team of top ministers and high Government officials was eagerly awaiting some message, and the telephone rang, 'Shakti is successful', said the excited voice of A.P.J. Abdul Kalam from the Alpha range near Pokhran. All were thrilled, their eyes became bright. This small group at PM's residence had enough to cheer about. They had taken India into the restricted circle of nuclear weapon states (P-5), although the notice at the door said, 'No Entry'.

President of India extended his falicitations to all the scientists and the technologists who collectively made this possible. In the true spirit of Buddha's smile he told the world that India had always stood for a peaceful world without nuclear weapons and this achievement would enable it to make a more effective contribution to the objective of complete and comprehensive disarmament and non-discriminatory and more equal order.

The thunder of Pokhran reached Cairo where G-15 countries were meeting in a summit. The last word at G-15 summit—not counting President Hosni Mubarak's 'Shukhran'—Krishan Kant, Vice-President, who emphasized that India's nuclear tests came in the wake of two dozen years of tremendous restraint and responsibility. If certain sections of the international community would ignore this and impose sanctions 'India will face it.' The collective wisdom of G-15 non-nuclear nations tended toward silence on this issue. (That is, they did not join the American tune of condemnation). The random opinion poll conducted in the city of Cairo brought forward such comments as,

"At last a friend of the Arabs is a nuclear power,"

"It is good, Egypt can now turn to India for support",

"It's Okay, but can a poor country like India afford the luxury?"

Those who Were Annoyed With Smiling Buddha: In 1974, Pakistan had called India's pne "A blackmail by India". This time, the country fumed and vowed to retaliate. It felt immediate and grave threats to Islamabad's security. On both the occasions, the same foreign powers reacted with identical irascibility and irrationality. These were New Zealand, Australia and Canada, all under the US Nuclear Umbrella. *These countries themselves were sitting under the shadow of nuclear umbrella and asking India to sit in the Sun*. They made tough statements and gestures against India. This time these three countries recalled their high commissioners for consultations. The ex-imperial British sluggishly followed their erstwhile colonials in sending their high commissioners to London for a summer break. The five permanent members of UN Security Council, P-5 countries made a public display of their displeasure, caused by India's muscling into their preserve: the Nuclear Club. But France and Russia went along with them somewhat unenthusiastically. Japan, in 1974, had merely regretted India's action, as Japan claimed to be opposed to all nuclear tests by any nation, for any reason, anywhere. This time Japan may deny/postpone India credits and aids.

The worst commentary about India's explosions appeared in American press. In 1974, the immediate American response had been adverse. Over the weeks this became bitter and later turned into impatience, even a desire to hurt. This time the US government, particularly the state department, used harsh and un-parliamentary language against India. The American people could not digest India's five nuclear explosions who have themselves conducted more than thousand explosions. Many articles appearing in American press speak of a recidivist and revanchist mood, flogging the usual clinched images—*Snake Charmers,Fakirs,Sati and Kipling*.

A cartoon shows a snake charmer blowing pipe before a flat basket, named India, and instead of snake, it is the explosion smoke coming out of the basket. The New York Times story on India was accompanied by reproduction of a painting of Lord Shiva, the creator and destroyer, with five heads, ten arms and a garland of skulls.

Reactions from Abroad (in details): Reactions from abroad started immediately after the tests were advertised. On June 6, the United Nations Security Council adopted resolution 1172 condemning the Indian tests (and that of Pakistan's). The US issued a strong statement condemning India and promised that sanctions would follow. The American establishment was embarrassed as there had been a serious intelligence failure in detecting the preparations for the tests. The UN also issued a statement expressing its disappointment. Canada, which had earlier supplied the Cirus nuclear reactor to India which was the source of Plutonium for the 1974 test, reassured the world that the Cirus reactor was not in any way connected in the 1998 tests. In keeping with its preferred approach to foreign policy in recent decades, the US imposed economic sanctions of India as punishment. In fact a 1994 anti-proliferation law made such sanction virtually automatic.

China issued a vociferous condemnation calling upon the international community to exert pressure on India to sign the Non-Proliferation Treaty (NPT) and eliminate its nuclear arsenal. With India joining the group of countries possessing nuclear weapons, a new strategic dimension had emerged in Asia, particularly South Asia.

Most other nations refrained from joining the US in imposing an economic embargo. Since most nations are not imposing similar sanctions, and India's exports and imports together constitute only 4% of its GDP, with US trade being only 10% of this total, the overall effect on India's economy from a direct trade embargo was small. For more significant were the restrictions on lending imposed by the US and its representatives on international finance bodies.

The most vehement reaction to India's nuclear tests was Pakistan's. Great ire was raised in Pakistan, which issued a severe statement blaming India for instigating a nuclear arms race in the region. After the first test Ayub Khan said that the Asian subcontinent has been thrust into a nuclear arms race and indicated that Pakistan was ready to conduct a nuclear test of its own. "We are prepared to match India. We have the capability...... We in Pakistan will maintain a balance with India in all fields," he said in an interview. "We are in a headlong arms race in the subcontinent." This time, Prime Minister Mohammad Nawaz Sharif vowed that his country would give a suitable reply to the Indians. The Pakistan Atomic Energy Commission (PAEC) carried out 5 underground nuclear tests at the Chagai test site at 3:16 PM (PST) on the afternoon of May 28, 1998, just 15 days after India's last test. (The yield of the tests was reported to be 40 kiloton. The US president Bill Clinton condemned these Pakistan's tests and said, "Two wrongs don't make a right."

However, other nations, such as Israel, France and Russia did not condemn India's tests. Israel issued a statement praising India's tests and declaring that India's reasons for carrying out nuclear tests were the same as Israel's.

❑

7

India and Disarmament

> ***"India had always stood for and worked for a peaceful world without nuclear weapons and this achievement would enable it to make a more effective contribution to the objective of complete and comprehensive disarmament and a non-discriminating and more equal order."***
>
> ***— President K.R. Narayanan.***

According to the International Peace Research Institute at Stockholm, there is a total stock of 1,000 metric ton Plutonium and 1,300 ton enriched Uranium in the world. Out of this, 80% material is possessed by only P-5 countries—America, Russia, England, France and China. A very large number of nuclear bombs can be made from this stock.

Universal Peace Symbol designed by Gerald Holtom in 1958

How to Save the Humanity? The world can be saved from the nuclear holocaust only when all the Weapons of Mass Destruction present anywhere in the world are completely destroyed. In any case nuclear weapons should not be allowed with the countries that procure them not for their security reasons but for some other impulsive reasons. These weapons must not be in the hands of countries or persons with weak mind.

We know during the days of *Mahabharata* some persons with immature mind had procured *Brahmastras* (weapons of mass destruction). Lord Krishna, committed to establish the rule of law, managed to destroy them before they could be misused. One such example is that of *Barbarik*, the grand son of mighty Bhim. Krishna did not take even a minute to behead the young man when he came to know that this emotional boy of impulsive nature possesses three Brahmastra *(Agneyastra, Vayavastra and Varunastra)*, each of which alone could destroy the life on entire earth.

Hurdles before Disarmament: Just look at the present time situation:

Pakistan is the only nuclear power where the military has its finger on the *nuclear button.* Its National Command Authority (NCA) formed on February 2, 2000 is headed by a General (Musharraf at that time), and is responsible for both development and deployment of Pakistan's nuclear weapons. The entire Pakistan's history of 64 years shows that whenever some democratic administration came into power, it has been eventually overthrown by its military, that too inspired by its religious fanatic sentiments.

The Sunday Times, quoting its senior White House adviser, reports that during Kargil Conflict, 1999, the Pakistan army had mobilized its nuclear arsenal against India, without the knowledge of their own Prime Minister Nawaz Sharif.

Terrorist Groups: Russian President Valadimir Putin expressed fears about the safety of Islamabad's nuclear arsenal. His fears are not unfounded. The whole of Pakistan region is very rapidly coming under the influence of Talibans and Osama-bin-

Laden, leader of the dreaded terrorist group Al Qaeda, who is considered to be the person behind 9/11 (September 11, 2001) disaster in America. Al Qaeda's designs are horrific. Recently, the US has interrogated Abu Zubaydah, a key lieutenant of Osama. Zubaydah revealed that Al Qaeda members are planning to construct a radiological bomb (Dirty Bomb), a conventional bomb fortified with radioactive material to attack a US nuclear power plant. Just think where a Krishna will come from to control such a situation?

Chilling Hoax: On November 15, 2002 the Hong Kong based Asia Times Online put out a *Chilling Interview* with Al Qaeda's No. 3 leader on its website. It revealed a horrific Al Qaeda's plot which in terms of scale and impact would have put 9/11 to shame. For, the target this time was to be not just a tower or a government establishment, but seven of the US's largest cities—all to be raised by nukes. Relief came when hours after this the website pulled the material out with a profuse apology under the caption, '*The Big Hoax—We fell for it*'.

Ex-Soviet Republics: Another danger to disarmament is a number of poorly supervised defence production facilities in various ex-Soviet republics, which would upgrade older weapons to create a new technological threat. Kazakhistan was a major site for Soviet-era Biological warfare production and atomic weapons testing.

The poorly supervised war factories may still be providing rogue regimes with even the means to make biological and nuclear arms. The US has charged Ukrane of black market $100 million sale of far advanced radar stations '*Kolchuga*' to Iraq. Unlike conventional radars, the Kolchuga emits no radar pulse, but works by passively scanning the signals given off by incoming aircraft. The US fears the unit could help Iraqi air defences survive an attack, because American anti-radar weapons work by homing in on radar beams.

Rogue Scientist: In 2004, the Pakistan's Metallurgist, Abdul Qadeer Khan, who was twice decorated with the Nation's highest civilian award, *Nishan-i-Imtiaz* (in 1996 and 1998) and is known as the Father of the Islamic Bomb sold nuclear secrets in the

International market triggering a global worry about loose nukes in wrong hands. A group of scientists led by Dr. A.Q. Khan, proliferated nuclear technology to North Korea, Libya and Iran.

During a period of six years (between 1997 and 2002) A.Q Khan secretly made 13 trips to North Korea and swapped centrifuge design and components for Uranium enrichment. In return he brought for Pakistan, 12 nuclear capable Nodong ballistic missiles, later renamed as Ghauri.

Warhead designs and other components were sold to Libya by Khan and his team between 1991 and 1997 through what, a UN nuclear inspector Dr. Mohamed El Baradei describes as '*the Wal-Mart* of private sector proliferation', for $50 million. This was revealed by the US when Libyan leader Colonel Muammar el-Gaddafi admitted that his country had been purchasing a Weapon of Mass Destruction (WMD) and agreed to dismantle them and subject them to International Inspections.

During 1989-91 Khan supplied centrifuges for enriching weapon grade Uranium and weapon related designs to Iran. This was revealed when UN inspectors probed into Iran's nuclear program and visited the facilities at Nikanj and Kalay Electric Complex in Iran.

Self-Imposed Disarmament: The rightful possessor of Brahmastra (WMD), as we mentioned earlier, is only one who, like Lord Rama and Arjun and not like Ashuathama can keep his mind and heart balanced and uses the Brahmastra only when it is unavoidable, that is, when it becomes imperative to save humanity and to maintain the law of the land. The only cure to eliminate the annihilation of life on earth is that these horrible weapons of mass destruction should be destroyed completely before a '*weak mind's*' hand reaches the button on the *Nuclear Table* and smashes the world. That is, every country should adopt *Self-Imposed Disarmament*. The initiative to destroy all the nuclear weapons should have come from the P-5 countries, particularly from US which have more nuclear arms than the total of other four countries and its own nuclear stock alone can destroy whole of world more than 15 times.

Former US President Jimmy Carter, Nobel Peace Prize winner for 2002 rightly said, "*One of the things that the US Government has not done is to comply with and enforce international efforts targeted to prohibit the arsenal of biological weapons that we ourselves have.*" He called for disarmament by Washington, which has taken the lead in urging such countries as North Korea and Iraq to destroy their Weapons of Mass Destruction.

The Barter Deal and Judo Diplomacy: North Korea is growing as another headache to disarmament efforts. In1990's North Korea started its own active program for nuclear weapons and even other Weapons of Mass Destruction. Being a signatory to the Non-Proliferation Treaty (NPT), Pyongyang (capital of North Korea) was not supposed to have a nuclear program. When in 1994, Washington confronted Pyongyang with proof of the latter's atomic ambitions, it refused to let International Atomic Energy Agency (IAEA) inspectors into its nuclear facilities and, in fact, almost went to war with the US. The tense stand-off ended only when the Korean pledged to desist from their nuclear program in return for the US agreeing to supply them with a couple of proliferation-proof nuclear reactors, oil and food supplies.

But the matter did not stop here. North Korea, on one hand, kept increasing secretly its nuclear activity by indulging in a *Barter Deal* with Pakistan and, on other hand, using her nuclear weapon program in balance of power politics.

According to American Intelligence, Pakistan was a major supplier of critical equipment for North Korea's clandestine nuclear weapon program. The equipment, which includes gas centrifuges used to create weapon-grade Uranium, appears to have been part of a barter deal beginning into the late 1990's in which North Korea supplied Pakistan with medium to long range missiles it could use to counter India's nuclear arsenal. What we have here is a perfect meeting of interests—the North Korea had what the Pakistan needed, and the Pakistan had a way for Kim Jong-II to restart a nuclear program he had stopped. As we know Dr. Abdul Qadir Khan, father of Pakistan's nuclear bomb, visited North Korea 13 times during 1992-1994 and did the initial negotiations.

According to B. Raman, former head of Research and Analysis Wing (RAW) Pakistan desk since 1998, "Pakistani nuclear scientists have been working in North Korea and North Korean missile experts in Pakistan."

Another incidence proves the Pyongyang-Pakistan nexus. In June, 1998, a North Korean diplomat in Islamabad had been murdered. Indian intelligence agencies suspect she paid the price for passing on vital information on what was going on. Her husband, Kang Thae-yun, was the local representative of Changgwang Sinyong, the key supplier of missile components to Pakistan and Iran.

In 1998, a Commission on missile threats, led by Donald Rumsfeld, who latar became the US Defence Secretary, concluded that North Korea, among other countries, was a major proliferator of missile technology to Pakistan and Iran. The Commission said in 1998, Pakistan tested its version of a North Korean designed Nodong, a missile with a range of 700 mile. Around the same time in 1997 or 1998, North Korea started her highly enriched Uranium project.

In July, 2002, in full view of American spy satellites, Pakistan used an American built C-130 cargo aircraft to land at a North Korean airfield and took on ballistic missile parts it needs to build a nuclear arsenal capable of reaching every strategic site in India. Meanwhile, North Korea had set up a second nuclear weapon program with Pakistani technology. The annoyed America and its allies suspended annual petroleum shipment to pressurise North Korea to give up this new program. As a tactical move on December 12, 2002, North Korean Foreign Minister said that its country would immediately reactivate the old Soviet nuclear reactor at Yongbyon and resume construction of other nuclear facilities it had stopped under the 1994 agreement. To increase pressure further, North

Korea on December 23, 2002, began removing United Nations seals from a nuclear laboratory used for extracting weapon-grade Plutonium from spent fuel rods. A source close to IAEA said, "North Koreans are cutting the seals of the nuclear fuel reprocessing laboratory." The North Korean spokesperson said, "Our country faced an immediate problem in electricity generation because the US has virtually abandoned its obligations."

Analysts say that North Korea is trying to force the US back to the negotiating table. It has tried such tactics before in a style dubbed as '*Judo Diplomacy*'.

All Efforts by India Went in Vain: Efforts were mooted to create an atmosphere of nuclear disarmament. In 1954, India mooted a move to ban nuclear testing. Again in 1963, India amongst other countries signed the *Partial Test Ban Treaty (PTBT)*, which prohibited testing of nuclear devices in the open. India could have made atom bomb as far back as 1956 but it did not. This sacrifice, however, did not assure the suspicion of the US. The first American sanctions against India were in place by 1957. But India did not go for nuclear tests even after Indo-China War in 1962 and border conflict with Pakistan in 1965. In a talk broadcast over All India Radio on UN Day in 1964, Dr. Homi Bhabha emphasized the need for the creation of a climate favourable to the countries which have the capabilities of making Atomic Bomb but have voluntarily refrained from doing so. But the pleas of the Indian scientific community and the defence establishment went in vain. India and other well meaning countries could not stop the nuclear weapon proliferation. United States and Russia still retain a nuclear arsenal of 9,000 and 7,000 warheads respectively. Britain and France despite being under the US nuclear umbrella maintain a small but deadly nuclear arsenal. Even Germany is keen to have a nuclear button. China has a deterrent of 450 nuclear warheads. Selig Harrison, a South Asian expert wrote, "If we try to preserve nuclear status *quo*, first India and then Japan will become overt nuclear weapon powers; not only because they face the Chinese nuclear arsenal, but also because they would not accept second class status. Both of them are capable of making ICBM that can reach the US."

Other Efforts for Disarmament: *Nuclear disarmament refers to both the act of reducing or eliminating nuclear weapons and to the end state a nuclear-free world in which these weapons are completely eliminated.*

Proponents of nuclear disarmament say that it would lessen the probability of nuclear war occurring, especially accidentally, while critics of nuclear disarmament say that it would undermine deterrence. Major nuclear disarmament groups include: ***Campaign for Nuclear Disarmament, and Green Peace and International Physicians for the Prevention of War***. There have been many large Anti-Nuclear demonstrations and protests.

In 1954, a letter in the Bulletin of Atomic Scientists was the start of a successful compaign to stop the Atomic Energy Commission dumping radioactive waste in the sea 19 km from Boston.

In 1962, Linus Pauling won the Nobel peace prize for his work to stop the atmospheric testing of nuclear weapons, and the 'Ban the Bomb' movement spread.

In 1963, many countries ratified the Partial Test Ban Treaty (PTBT) prohibiting atmospheric nuclear testing. Radioactive fall out became less of an issue and the nuclear disarmament movement went into decline for some years.

On June12, 1982, one million people demonstrated in New York City's central park against nuclear weapons and for an end to the Cold War (between the US and Soviet Union) arms race. It was the largest anti-nuclear protest and the largest political demonstration in American history. US President Ronald Reagan had 'a world free of nuclear weapons' as his personal mission. He changed the name 'SALT—Strategic Arms Limitation Talks' to 'START—Strategic Arms Reduction Talks'.

On June 20, 1983, International day of Nuclear disarmament protests were held at 50 sites across the United States.

In 1986, hundreds of people walked from Los Angeles to Washington DC in the Great Peace March for Global Nuclear Disarmament.

During 1980s and 1990s, there were many Nevada Desert Experience protests and peace camps at the Nevada Test sites.

On May 1, 2005, 40,000 anti-nuclear/anti war protesters marched past the United Nations in New York, 60 years after the atomic bombing of Hiroshima and Nagasaki. This was the largest anti-nuclear rally in the U.S. for several decades.

In Britain there were many protests about the movement's proposal to replace the aging Trident weapons system with a newer model. The largest protest had 100,000 participants and, according to polls, 59% of the public opposed the move.

The International Conference on Nuclear Disarmament took place in Oslo in February, 2008, and was organised by the Government of Norway, the Nuclear Threat Initiative and the Hoover Institute. The conference was entitled achieving the Vision of a World free of Nuclear Weapons and had the purpose of building consensus between nuclear weapon states and non-nuclear weapon states in relation to the nuclear Non-Proliferation Treaty (NPT).

Test Ban Treaties: Arms control advocates had campaigned for the adoption of a treaty banning all nuclear explosions since the early 1950's, when public concern was aroused as a result of radioactive fall-out from atmospheric nuclear tests and escalating arms race. Over 50 nuclear explosions were registered between July16, 1945, when the first nuclear explosive test was conducted by US at Alamogordo, New Mexico, and December 31, 1953. Indian Prime Minister Pandit Jawahar Lal Nehru voiced the heightened international concern in 1954, when he proposed the elimination of all nuclear test explosions worldwide. However, within the context of the Cold War, skepticism about the compatibility to verify compliance with a comprehensive nuclear test ban treaty posed a major obstacle in any agreement.

When the extreme danger intrinsic to Nuclear War and the

possession of nuclear weapons became apparent to all sides during the Cold War, a series of disarmament and non-proliferation treaties were agreed upon between the US, the Soviet Union and several other states throughout the world. Many of these treaties involved years of negotiations, and seemed to result in important steps toward creating a nuclear weapons free world.

The P-5 countries and those under American nuclear umbrella signed Non-Proliferation Treaty (NPT). Important aims of NPT are to tackle disarmament, non-proliferation and peaceful use of nuclear energy. The NPT also uses a cut-off date of 1968 to establish who is or is not Nuclear Weapon State. Looking at the hegemonic attitude of nuclear powers and security risk India took the plunge in 1974. But this test proved to be an empty gesture. It achieved only the stoppage of heavy water supply from Canada.

India and the US were the original co-sponsors of Conference on Disarmament held in Geneva in 1994, which talked of a ban on nuclear testing. But the NPT failed in its aims particularly in tackling the disarmament. China which had already signed the NPT and CTBT (Comprehensive Test Ban Treaty) proliferated the nuclear weapons by helping Pakistan and other few countries in making nuclear weapons and developing missiles. Even US transferred Advanced Missile Technology to China, where China used this technology to improve the reliability of its own ballistic missiles which could then be used against America itself. Only one country has been known to ever dismantle their nuclear arsenal completely—the apartheid government of South Africa apparently developed half a dozen crude fission weapons during the 1980's, but they were dismantled in the early 1990's. Libya, a non-nuclear weapon state, party to the NPT also acknowledged and eliminated past nuclear weapons program.

At this India became a bit cautious. After the permanent and indefinite extension of NPT in May 1995, India linked the signing of the CTBT with a time bound plan for Global disarmament and so did not sign the CTBT. India's security needs have increasingly called for nuclear deterrence. So India performed five nuclear tests in May 1998 with different yields covering the full range right from sub-kiloton to 45 kiloton or more, including the thermonuclear device. India also continued to increase the strike range of its missile—Agni.

India had never made bones about its deep distrust of loopholes marred CTBT which proposes an immediate end to underground nuclear testing, but not to existing nuclear arsenals. With nuclearised potential enemies glaring across the country's Northern and Western frontiers, India cannot afford to try and win hearts and minds in the west by forging the only effective deterrent available to the nation.

List of Key Treaties: Following is the list of important treaties agreed upon by various countries from time to time.

PTBT—1963: The Partial Test ban Treaty prohibits all testing of nuclear weapons except underground.

NPT—1968: The Non-Proliferation Treaty has three main pillars—non-proliferation, disarmament, and the right to peaceful use of nuclear technology. Under this treaty non-nuclear weapon states were prohibited from, inter alia, possessing, manufacturing or acquiring nuclear weapons or other nuclear explosive devices. All signatories (currently with 189 member states) including nuclear weapon states, were committed to the goal of total nuclear disarmament.

However, nations like India have not ratified NPT on grounds that such a treaty is fundamentally discriminatory as it places limitations on states that do not have nuclear weapons while making no efforts to curb weapons development by declared nuclear weapon states.

SALT-I-1972: Strategic Arms Limitation Talks is an Interim Agreement on offensive Arms. The Soviet Union and The US agreed to freeze in the number of ICBMs and SLBMs that they would deploy.

ABM-1972: According to Anti-Ballistic Missile treaty, the US and Soviet Union could deploy ABM interceptors at two sites, each with up to 100 ground-based launchers for ABM interceptor missiles. In 1974 protocol, the US and SU agreed to only deploy an ABM system to one site.

SALT-II-1979: Replacing SALT-I, SALT-II limits both the US and SU to an equal number of ICBM launchers and heavy bombers. Also places limits on MIRV (Multiple Independent Re-entry Vehicles).

INF-1987: Intermediate-range Nuclear Forces treaty created a global ban on short- and long-range nuclear weapons systems as well as an intrusive verification regime.

START-I-1991: This treaty limits long range nuclear forces in the United States and the newly independent states of the former Soviet Union to 6000 attributed warheads on 1600 ballistic missiles and bombers.

START-II-1993: This was a bilateral agreement between the US and Russia which attempted to commit each side to deploy not more than 3000 to 3500 warheads by December, 2007 and also included a prohibition against deploying MIRV on ICBMs. But this agreement was never put into force.

SORT-2002: Under the Strategic Offensive Reduction Treaty, also known as Moscow Treaty, Russia and the US agreed to reduce their 'Strategic Nuclear Warheads' (a term that remain undefined in the treaty) to between 1700 and 2200 by 2012.

CTBT-1996: The Comprehensive Test Ban Treaty is an International Treaty which bans all nuclear explosions in all environments, for military or civilian purposes. It was adopted by the UN General Assembly on September 10, 1996, but not yet entered into force

Article 1: Each state party undertakes not to carryout any nuclear weapon test explosion or any other nuclear explosion, and to prohibit and prevent any such nuclear explosion at any place under its jurisdiction or control.

Article 2: Each state party undertakes, furthermore, to refrain from causing, encouraging, or in any way participating

in the carrying out of any nuclear weapon test explosion or any other nuclear explosion.

Currently 181 states have signed and 148 states have ratified. China, Egypt, Indonesia, have not yet signed it.

New START treaty signed in 2010, but not yet ratified by either Russia or by the US.

UN Security Council: In UN Security council meeting called to condemn nuclear tests by India (and Pakistan), all the non-nuclear members openly criticized the permanent five countries (P-5) strongly. Their feeling was that the willfully inadequate response by the five in implementing their NPT obligations to disarm, and their selective approach to disarmament had contributed to the current explosions (by India and Pakistan). One country said, "Having one set of rules for some and another for others cannot be justified. The world would have been a much safer place if we all played according to the same rules. This discrimination, at the global level, is epitomized by the possession of over 30,000 nuclear weapons in the hands of the five states, which they claim, they will retain indefinitely."

America and other countries must consider the point that India has not violated any norms, legal obligations or political commitment in undertaking the nuclear tests. China and France also continued to test in gross violation of their commitments and assurances. As things stand, any future tests by India would also not break any laws or norms. As far as CTBT is concerned, India has categorically stated that it will not accept this treaty in its present (discriminatory) form. In fact, it is the nature and method of finalizing the CTBT which had pushed India into undertaking the five tests (in 1998) to prove the credibility of its capability.

Non-Aligned Movement: In the 12th Non-Aligned movement (NAM) summit, on September 2, 3, 4, 1998, India achieved a milestone on the path of disarmament. India made it absolutely clear to the member nations that the nuclear test series conducted by it should not be considered as an act of proliferation.

It moved a resolution to hold an International Conference on Disarmament in 1999, with the objective of arriving at an agreement on a phased program for the complete elimination of nuclear weapons. India also promised to this conference to discontinue nuclear tests and not transfer nuclear weapon related technology to any other country. It is a good symptom that India's call for nuclear disarmament, as also the need to combat global terrorism under the broad frame work of the UN charter, have found full support with NAM.

The Changing Global Strategic Framework: [From 'A New Nuclear Idiom' written by Brahma Chellaney: Hindustan Times (21-3-2002)]

Having been a target of non-proliferation-related sanctions and exclusion, India should be pleased that global developments are beginning to run counter to much of the traditional wisdom on non-proliferation. The old thing is giving way to attitudes pivoted more openly on national interests.

The US leadership is not shy to discard or block arms-control mechanism it considers outdated or detrimental to US interests, be it Biological Weapon Convention verification, ABM Treaty, START process or CTBT. The US missile defences, which hold coded benefits for India, are an open challenge to the existing nuclear framework. Washington is seeking to move from a universal to differentiated non-proliferation policy. There are indications that President Bush (the then US President) team wished to distinguish between proliferators that threaten US interests and those that seek nuclear weapons merely to address regional insecurities in a non-provocative manner. At a time when the US strategy towards China is based on hedging, Washington cannot dismiss the role India's modest deterrent could play to bring stability and equilibrium in Asia.

Although, it may still be impolitic to officially acknowledge it, the *US has tacitly accepted India as a Nuclear Weapon State*. The growing acceptance of India's nuclear weapon status is a sore point with China. Its interlocutors bristle at the Russian proposal for Non-First-Use (NFU) obligations in an India-Russia-China framework. In Beijing's view, such a trilateral arrangement, based on India's and China's unilateral NFU policies and the Sino-Russian bilateral NFU accord, could amount to India's backdoor entry in the Nuclear Club.

China's unstable, terror-breeding ally, Pakistan, represents a unique (and disquieting) nuclear case. But it may be possible to accommodate India and Israel, with their support for non-proliferation norms and responsible conduct, within the NPT regime. This can be done enlisting them as members of the NPT's subsidiary arrangements (such as the Nuclear Suppliers' Group) without making them enter the inner ring—NPT 'Sanctum Sanctorium'. This appears the only way to preserve the troubled regime.

Nuclear weapons will continue to play a critical role because they possess unique properties. While the gap between Russian and Chinese nuclear forces is set to considerably narrow, the Sino-Indian asymmetry will only widen. India does not have to qualitatively or quantitatively match Chinese capabilities for achieving credible deterrence, but it needs to speed up development of second strike assets.

While the future of Pakistan's nuclear weapons seems uncertain, this nuclear flasher no longer has the space, under US military presence, to flash a nuclear threat at India. In China's case, with nationalism serving as a substitute for declining ideology, nuclear weapons are bound to assume a greater security and power-projection role.

India's Intentions: The day India conducted Pokhran, 1998, it expressed its commitment to the Chemical Weapon Convention and the Biological Weapon Convention. It also offered to participate in the negotiations for the Fissile Material Cut-off Treaty (FMCT) in the Geneva based Conference on Disarmament. India's principled stand on NPT, CTBT, and FMCT have forced the P-5 to find ways of accommodating Indian interests. It is possible to restore that status even while claiming to be a Nuclear Weapon State. The pressure on the P-5 can then be maintained to move forward on disarmament and Indian security needs. It will require using the negotiating value of nuclear weapons instead of their deterrent value. India will find bigger pay-offs in that exercise and in the process evolve a new meaning to nuclear weapons. That will be the real test of India's strategic thinking.

Making India's intentions very clear, President K.R. Narayanan said on the success of Operation Shakti, "India had always stood for and worked for a peaceful world without nuclear weapons and this achievement would enable it to make a more effective contribution to the objective of complete and comprehensive disarmament and a non-discriminating and more equal order."

❑

8

Economic Sanctions

> ***"International finance has become so interdependent and so interwoven with trade and industry that....political and military powers can in reality do nothing. It should be kept in mind, that no foreign businessman can ignore the potential of the vast Indian market. This is a guarantee that the country will shortly overcome the short term impact of the economic sanctions."***
>
> ***—Norman Angells, in his famous book 'The Great Allusions'.***

For many years, the five nuclear powers have advised the rest of the world t*o do not as they do, but do as they say*. By permanently extending the nuclear Non-Proliferation Treaty, they have safeguarded their nuclear monopoly for good. So when India defiantly conducted nuclear tests, their sense of affront prompted them to apply sanctions against India and to get sweeping non-implementable resolutions passed by the UN Security Council, the Group of Eight (G-8) nations and their own Permanent-Five (P-5) club.

After Pokhran 1998, the US and a number of India's major trading partners imposed economic sanctions. However, US economic sanctions were lifted or eased within a few months of their imposition and Congress gave the President the authority to remove all remaining restrictions in 1999. The sanctions were lifted incrementally. President Bush issued a final determination on September 22, 2001, to remove the remaining sanctions against India.

Generally, Economic Sanctions might be defined as coercive economic measures taken by one country against one or more countries for a variety of reasons, to force a change in policies, or at least to demonstrate a country's opinion about the others' policies. Economic sanctions include, but are not limited to *tariffs, trade barriers, import duties, import-export quotas, denial of foreign assistance, loans and investments, or control of foreign assets and economic transactions.* The most famous example of an economic sanction is the fifty years' US embargo against Cuba.

UN Resolutions: Practically speaking the UN Security Council resolution against Pokhran explosions cannot harm India much. Every year several major resolutions are approved by the UN General Assembly, only to be scorned by the great powers. With the P-5 in-charge of disarmament and the Security Council, the UN cannot implement its own resolutions, including its very first in 1946 which mandated 'The elimination of atomic weapons from national armaments.'

Summit by G-8 Countries: The nuclear powers could not succeed in their efforts to convince all the G-8 countries. These eight developed countries are Britain, Canada, France, Germany, Italy, Japan, United States and Russia. The summit called by G-8 at Birmingham just after Pokhran 1998 sensibly was not unanimus on sanctions against India. During summit deliberations even President Clinton had to admit that India had been neglected for far too long. There is little doubt that two factors contributed to this neglect: first, the drive by Americans and also the Western World to legitimise the possession of nuclear weapons only in the hands of the Big Five and secondly, their preoccupation with Pakistan from the days of the Cold War. Now that India has demonstrated its nuclear prowess, they have realized that India is really concerned with the Sino-Pakistani military cooperation. They also realized the blatant unjustifiability of the Big Five retaining their monopoly of nuclear weapons while loftily advising others to refrain from acquiring them.

An editorial in *Hindustan Times*, May 19, 1998 sums up the reasons of not recommending sanctions against India in this summit as follows:

1. The sanctions are really effective as with the fear that such a move will hurt the Western companies as well. So they opted for self interest instead of a fake moral posture.
2. The globalization process to which India at present appears more committed than before the explosions, is evidently acting as a disincentive to the imposition of sanctions.
3. India's size, its potential as a market and its success as an open society.
4. India remains the best and only judge of its defence requirements in a dangerous neighbourhood.
5. Even earlier, countries like France, Britain and Russia had made it clear that sanctions were not in their minds.
6. India's nuclear tests have received support not only within the country but elsewhere too, as in the Arab World, where it has evidently been interpreted as a rebuff to American double standards.

Most of all, India has already launched a diplomatic offensive to convince the world that it remains a responsible player on the world scene committed to universal disarmament and ready to go the extra mile for the sake of peace in the world.

Rethinking on Economic Sanctions: Fortunately by self realization, and by India's efforts through its special envoy Jaswant Singh, there is a great reflection and introspection in America. Many in that country now wonder, "Has our reaction been too hasty and too harsh? The US now has realized the following:

India did not sign the NPT because it was discriminatory, but also because the treaty meant that, "China, the internally oppressive and undemocratic occupying force on India's border would be permitted to have nuclear weapons whereas India would be denied any recourse to such weapons."

India had never been a proliferator of nuclear weapons and missiles, but China a nuclear power had done so time and again. According to some estimates, 90 % of China's weapons sale went to states on the border of India. Chinese proliferation of weapons and technologies to Pakistan are of particular concern. The Centre for Non-Proliferation Studies at the Monterey Institute had a detailed chronology of Pakistani nuclear development with active assistance from China, in violation of NPT. In 1983, China supplied Pakistan with enough highly enriched Uranium for one to two nuclear weapons. China also supplied complete design of a 25 kiloton nuclear bomb. In September, 1986 Pakistan conducted 'Cold Tests' of a nuclear implosion device at Chagai. In 1990, China provided assistance for the construction of the Chashma Plutonium reprocessing facility. Against clear violation of the missile technology control regime, Beijing also collaborated with Islamabad's missile program.

After four years in September, 2002, US government's security strategy document, identifies India a potential great power and says that US has undertaken a transformation in its bilateral relationship with India based on conviction that US interests require a strong relationship with India. The document admits differences remain over India's nuclear and missile program and the pace of economic reforms. In the past, these may have dominated over thinking about India, today we start with a view of India, as a growing power with shared strategic interests.

Incidentally, P-5 countries are discovering that the international searchlight is increasingly focused on them, with many nations sharing the feeling that it is unfair to highlight India when P-5 themselves have not fulfilled their own obligations under Article 5 of the NPT to reduce and eliminate their own nuclear arsenal. The P-5 still possess enough nuclear weapons to destroy the planet several times over. But the fact that the P-5 felt the need to try to make the points was indicative of a major shift in their perceptions. The US public is taking serious note of Sino-American relations and the then President Clinton's policy towards China.

T.P. Sreenivasan, Deputy Chief of Mission at the Indian Embassy in Washington hopes, "*We shall be able to move towards a new kind of relationship with the United States which would on the one hand, guarantee that non-proliferation continues to the extent in this world in the sense that new countries will not acquire nuclear weapons, but at same time will be a recognition of India's own need to have a minimum deterrent*." India has made it very clear that its nuclear weapons capability is not a threat to any one. It has nothing to do with either China or Pakistan or with any kind of threat that we perceive but it has everything to do with the security of the future for a brilliant people.

Strategy to Counter Economic Sanctions: Actually, the weapon of sanctions is a two edged sword. It cuts both ways. Norman Angells writes in his famous book *The Great Allusions* that international finance has become so interdependent and so interwoven with trade and industry that.....political and military powers can in reality do nothing. It should be kept in mind that no foreign businessman can ignore the potential of the vast Indian market. This is a guarantee that the country will shortly overcome the short term impact of the economic sanctions.

With business interests dominating the industrialized West, the sanctions would hurt these investors more. For example, given India's high ratings as the largest borrower, funding agencies like the World Bank would have to think twice before altogether putting an end to the loan proposals.

India may aim at wooing fresh investors like Russia, France, UK among the G-8 states which did not take an extreme view of the nuclear tests.

The confident mood of the nation offers immense opportunity for kick starting the economy by more than making up to the damage due to sanctions. In fact the national euphoria can be channelised for making optimum mobilization of resources both from the country and from outside.

The Non-Resident Indians (NRIs) can be mobilized to come forward to help their Motherland with large funds. With an estimated annual saving of US $400 billion, the NRIs could pull the country out of the likely morass as a fallout from sanctions. At the same time India can bring to the country a portion of unaccounted fund lying abroad. More than US $100 billion are lying abroad. If both the NRIs and the Indian businessman can bring back only 5% of this money to help their Motherland at this hour of trial, this amount of US $ 5 billion will take care of short term impact of the sanctions.

❑

9

The Operation Shakti—A Short Story

> ***"The men watching the scene from the safe distance were amazed and horrified to see that a mond of earth the size of a cricket field was lifted by several meters. A viewer (scientist) spoke out, 'O yes, now I can believe the story of Lord Krishna lifting Goverdhan Mountain.' The earth was rocking with quake-like force. There was a terrifying rumbling sound all around. But jawans watching this dance of god of earth were thrilled. All of them broke out spontaneously, Bharat Mata ki Jai."***
>
> ***— From this book.***

It was a calm, quiet and dark night on May 1 at 3:00AM at Santa Cruz airport of Mumbai. The feeble pale fifth moon had set in western horizon. Rows of twinkling electric bulbs and headlights were trying to push the darkness away. There was no activity on the vast field of the airport. Few civilian planes were sleeping in the hangers at the outskirt. Suddenly, lights were switched on in an aeroplane parked at the far end. The AN-32 plane of IAF team DELTA was being readied for a secret and historic flight. Major General Natraj strode towards the DELTA plane. Following him were soldiers carrying about half a dozen wooden 'Apple Crates'. But these were too heavy to be apple crates. Inside each of these crates was a perfectly shaped ball of weapon grade Plutonium. The lead shields protecting these balls had made the crates much heavier. In order to make this secret mission appearing a simple activity, only a couple of sten-gun wielding commandos were guarding them under the command of Col. Umang Kapoor. A smart officer wearing spectacles with tinted glasses and metallic frame popularly known as Mamaji was supervising the mission. These jawans, in spite of being soldiers, were not walking in steps. Perhaps they did not want to wake up those sleeping in the distant hangers by synchronized sound of their steps.

The crates were loaded inside DELTA vehicle. The commandos occupied back seats. The officers sat in front seats. General Natraj waved the 'go ahead' signal to the pilot who was looking towards him from the cockpit window. The aircraft moved slowly on the strip, gradually gained speed and flew in the sky.

This quiet and small mission was a part of a great operation set up by the Government of India to test a few nuclear devices in the Pokhran range of Rajasthan. The scientists, technicians, engineers, army jawans and Indian Air Force (IAF) officers—all about 100 in number—had been working for the last 20 days to make the operation a success. But the success was not only in detonating these Weapons of Mass Destruction, but in keeping the movements and activities a top secret from the hovering spy-satellites and other spying agencies till the seismographs at different world observatories and intelligence centers recorded the explosions and shocked the world with the startling news of Great Indian Nuclear Blasts. Therefore, to prevent the leakage of the news of frequent visits by scientists, engineers etc., to Pokhran, all civilians had adopted assumed names and dressed in olive green fatigues. The four teams with their exclusive expertise were participating in this great operation code named 'SHAKTI'. BRAVO, a team from Department of Atomic Energy (DAE) was to contribute the bombs of small and big size—right from sub-kiloton yield to a 45 kiloton Hydrogen Bomb. CHARLIE, a team from Defence Research and Development Organization (DRDO) was to supply the new and reliable detonators, ruggedised fuses, the implosion assembly and safety checks. An Indian Army team ALPHA was deputed to maintain a number of 200 to 300 meter deep shafts, to provide transport and to camouflage the testing activity. The DELTA team from IAF was to provide the aircraft and helicopter service to move personnel, ferry the Plutonium and to monitor radioactivity after the implosion.

By now, the readers must have realised that the officers traveling in the DELTA AN-32 plane were actually not military men but some scientists. The officer disguised as Major General Natraj was actually Rajgopal Chidambaram, the chief designer of the Shakti round of tests and Chairman of India's Atomic Energy Commission (AEC). The name 'Natraj' perhaps was selected for him, because he was going to perform '*Tandav'—the dance of death* within few days like Lord Shiva (Natraj). Mamaji was nobody else but country's most brilliant engineer Anil Kakodhar, the then Director of Bhabha Atomic Research Centre (BARC) at Trombay.

****

The DELTA plane was scaling the sky. General Natraj asked Mamaji,

"Major! Are the 'Apples' in perfect shapes?"

"Yes, Sir," replied Mamaji.

"Our physicists and chemists have worked very hard to enrich the Plutonium metal to weapon grade, while our skilled engineers and technicians have wonderfully turned them into perfect spherical shapes, each weighing between 5 to 10 kg." The General felt satisfied. He smiled, "Are you so confident about the chaps at BARC?"

"Of course, Sir," replied Mamaji.

****

After two hours' journey the DELTA AN-32 landed at Jaisalmer military base. The officers swiftly came down the plane. A convoy of 4 trucks from ALPHA had already lined up to take this team and the apple-crates to the heart of Rajasthan desert—

Pokhran. The soldiers and the commandos, swang into action. They transferred the crates to one of the ALPHA trucks and the convoy sped up to destination. Though this journey was as hard, perspiring and tiring as any summer journey through a desert yet General Natraj felt very comfortable. Of course, the anxiety and excitement of doing one of the world's greatest experiments was the reason but General Natraj felt something more. He told Mamaji:

"During the last operation in 1974, the Plutonium crates were ferried by road instead of by air. By God, It was a harrowing journey from Trombay to Pokhran, lasting two sweating days through the desert. Till then our technology had not developed so much as to make the consignment so light as to be safely carried out by air. Being in-charge of the mission, I could not take chance and had to hop aboard the convoy of army trucks."

"Yes, I can realise that, Sir," said Mamaji, "Your team at DAE skillfully miniaturized the devices and crafted the weapons into compact size and shape. We all, at BARC, are very much amazed by your technical skills."

On reaching Pokhran two other officers, Major General Prithvi Raj and Major Srinivasan (Santy), welcomed them at the door of the 'Prayer Hall'—a temporary device preparation building in the range. The code name Major General Prithvi Raj was rightly attributed to Dr. A.P.J. Abdul Kalam, the Missile man of India, who spearheaded the country's missile program and developed Agni and Prithvi. Major Santy was nobody else but one K. Santhanam who had synergized the efforts of DAE and DRDO for making India a Nuclear Weapon State.

The Prayer hall, though, a make-shift Laboratory housed in a barrack, was alive with many scientists donned in military uniforms busy in mating various components of the nuclear devices. General Prithvi Raj told General Natraj that the package containing the conventional explosives, detonators, triggers and other material to assemble the nuclear devices had already been supplied by CHARLIE.

The men had been working in the open ground only during night and carried on till the small hours without any sleep. This was done to avoid detection by snooping satellites. Chances of detection in the night are zero and the quality of satellite images is very bad. General Prithvi Raj had given them only two day's time to complete five assemblies—Shakti-I to Shakti-V. One thermonuclear bomb, one fission bomb and three sub-kiloton bombs with 0.2, 0.5 and 0.3 kiloton yield respectively.

A nuclear Device Being Lowered in a Well at Midnight on May 8

Preparing for the Devices in the 'Deer Park', Col. Santy transfers the Firing key to the Range Safety Officer Vasudev

****

Next noon, May 2, when the two generals, two majors, and two others donned as captains were busy in deliberations in the control room temporarily set up in a well protected bunker, code named Deer Park, the wireless gave a flash. Major General Prithvi Raj received the message. There was sad news. The General looked very serious. All others looked at him with curiosity. The General looked at Mamaji and spoke in a choked voice, "Major! You leave this room immediately and proceed for home." Major was stunned. His heart beat increased. "Was he going to be Court-Martialled!" a thought flashed in his mind, but why? The General moved to Mamaji. He affectionately put his hand on Mamaji's shoulder and took him outside the control room. A hot breeze cooled their sweating bodies for a while. Prithv Raj said, "Mama, your father has left all of us and your family for ever. You are ordered by the Headquarter to reach your home immediately." Mama could not control himself. He burst into tears. He had lost his father. At the same time he was being deprived of the opportunity to have his life's most wonderful experiment of operation Shakti. He had always aspired to do something which he had never done earlier and also what others have not done. But now, when the destination was just a few days ahead, the destiny was dragging him away to his home! He looked at the General and murmured, "Sir......, "No, no," interrupted Prithvi Raj, "You have to fly home without loosing a minute. You must join the funeral. I hope you will forgive all of us for not joining you at this juncture."

"O.K....., Sir," said Mamaji, "But Sir, you promise me you will not pass on my duties to any one else. I will be back by tomorrow evening."

"That is like a brave son of a great father," said Prithvi Raj, "Don't worry. None of us will be able to enjoy the fruits of this great mission without you. You are an indispensable member of Operation Shakti. We all shall wait for you."

"Yes, yes," nodded other team-mates who had, meanwhile, come out of the control room and had listened their conversation. The General hugged Mamaji and patted his back to consol him. Minutes after, he was moving in an ALPHA vehicle towards Jaisalmer military air base.

****

All rushed back into the Deer Park. The 'Shakti' would not allow them to waste even a minute. They had to discuss and finalise many things.

"What will be the yield of Hydrogen Bomb to be tested?" asked

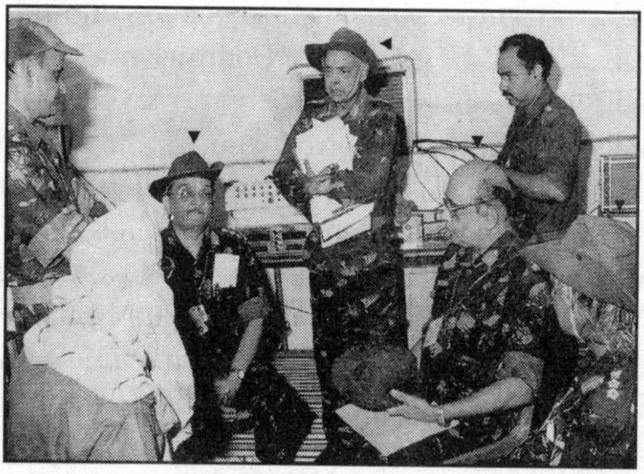

May 11: Consultations in the Control Room

Major Santy. General Natraj was already prepared with the answer. He took out a file containing a large number of data printed on computer stationary. He turned few pages of the file and said, "Sir, my BRAVO experts made precise calculations using computer simulation techniques. Keeping in view the location of villages around Pokhran, our calculations have reached a figure of 45 kiloton for the maximum energy which could safely be detonated. We have also calculated the amount of the fuel to be used and the depth to which the devices should be buried so as to prevent radioactivity from rising to the surface."

"All right, done," approved the Shakti team. General Prithvi Raj moved out towards the door, saying, "Let us inspect the Ground Zero." All others followed him.

A few square kilometer area of the wide field had been cordoned by barbed wires. Since the sun had set, it was time to work in the field. ALPHA jawans became busy with the task of dressing up the shafts in the ground to be used for nuclear tests.

There were five shafts in all. *White House,* a 200 meter deep shaft contained Hydrogen Bomb. Another 150 meter deep shaft named *Taj Mahal*, was assigned to the Fission Bomb, and the first sub-kiloton bomb was placed in a third one named *Kumbhkaran.* Other two shafts named *NT1 and NT2* were kept reserved to be used later. All the shafts were adequately camouflaged, lest the surveillance satellites should smell a foul.

Toward Ground Zero

Mamaji had returned and was working with full vigour to complete his backlog. In the night of May 9, he along with other scientists and engineers descended into the *Kumbhkaran* to carryout routine checks. Suddenly, electric power failed. It was complete dark in the well. The lift available to come out became dead. They were all trapped to spend about five hours in that dark well. Mamaji would not allow any one to get bored or terrified throughout this long period, till the power was restored. They finished the task and came out joking with each other. Such was the vigour and motivation for completing the mission that none of the soldiers reported sick throughout the month. Even Mamaji had no time to grieve.

****

Next night, jawans were working on the ground to seal the explosive chambers with cement and sand. A bulldozer was dancing around to push the material inside the shaft. Suddenly, a large boulder got a kick from the bulldozer and rolled dangerously towards the shaft. This would have crushed the nuclear device laid deep into the well, but for the timely courageous action of the ALPHA jawans. Like a falcon, a jawan pounced upon the boulder and clung to it. But the mass rolling on the sand was so heavy that it would drag the jawan along with it. The situation became more dangerous. But other two jawans, instantaneously jumped forward to hold on his legs. The mishap was saved. The boulder was thrown away. Everybody felt relieved.

****

At last, the D-day had come. All the workers had moved to safer distances after completing their jobs in the field. Major General Prithvi Raj along with his fellow officers was preparing for the great explosion in the Deer Park. He checked every computer and control panel fitted with green, orange and red buttons. He looked at the faces of his colleagues, winked his eyes to get their nod and moved a key to set the clock for countdown. This would have triggered a series of explosions and shocked the world, precisely at 9AM. But at 8AM, just an hour before the zero point, Captain Adi Marzban who was monitoring the weather as range meteorological officer, rushed into the control room. He was seemingly uncomfortable. Without bothering to salute the Generals he told them, "a high velocity wind has started blowing in a direction which could send any accidental radiation fallout from the blasts towards nearby villages. So we would have to put the mission 'On Halt' till the wind died down." All had to obey and respect the dictates of Pawan Dev— the god of wind.

All sat impassively till noon. It was very hot. The temperature sore to 45 degree Celsius. Some of the officers removed their Gorkha hats waved to evaporate the sweat streaming down their faces. Major General Natraj got lost in his past memories: Twenty four years back, in1974, he had participated in India's mission of a peaceful nuclear explosion. The memories of the first great experience thrilled him. He was eagerly looking again and again towards the key of the timer. Major General Prithvi Raj, on the other hand, was feeling helpless. The Prime Minister had given him 30 days time to complete the mission. Today, that period was just over when this unexpected weather problem tied their hands. He was restlessly moving in bunker like a lion in the cage. His Gorkha hat was too small to hide his silvery white hair spread around his neck which was giving the impression of a lion's mane.

Ultimately, by God's grace, the anxious moments were over. Captain Marzban from the range meteorological office informed that the wind had fallen silent around Pokhran. The glooming eyes of the 'lion' smiled. He proudly and confidently turned the timer on. At 3:45PM, a tiny electric current triggered the detonators.

Instantly, temperature around 300 metre deep inside the earth, rose to million degree Celsius—as high as temperature on the Sun. Within a fraction of a second the earth started Tandav. About 1000 ton of rocks were boiling. This lava rose in the sky like a mountain and vanished. Again, thousands of tons of rocks dripped down the crater formed by evaporated material. This molten rock suddenly cooled and trapped the radioactive radiations. The men watching the scene from the safe distance were amazed and horrified to see that a part of earth the size of a cricket field was lifted by several meters. A viewer (scientist) spoke out, "O yes, now I can believe the story of Lord Krishna lifting Goverdhan Mountain." The earth was rocking with quake-like force. There was a terrifying rumbling sound all around. But jawans watching this dance of god of earth were thrilled. All of them broke out spontaneously, 'Bharat Mata ki Jai'.

Bharat Mata ki Jai

Inside the Deer Park all the officers were extremely happy. The tickle was followed by a spontaneous eruption of joy among scientists after the tests were confirmed. Their mission was complete. They warmly congratulated and hugged each other. Chidambaram, Kakodkar, Santhanam and India's great missile man A.P.J. Abdul Kalam, all had a feeling of self-fulfilment, a feeling of having contributed to national security. There was a sense of collective jubilation rather than individual triumphalism. Dr kalam was absolutely delighted,and he complimented the team. He took off his Gorkha cap and his silvery mane fluttered in the desert air. He jumped towards the wireless set; dialed the Prime Minister's residence and cried with full voice, "Sir, Congratulations. The Operation Shakti is successful."

❑❑❑